DESTROYER AND PRESERVER

DESTROYER AND PRESERVER

Shelley's Poetic Skepticism

Lloyd Abbey

University of Nebraska Press
Lincoln and London

This book has been published with the help of a grant from the Canadian Federation for the Humanities, using funds provided by the Social Sciences and Humanities Research Council of Canada.

Library of Congress Cataloging in Publication Data

Abbey, Lloyd Robert, 1943–
 Destroyer and preserver.

 Includes bibliographical references and index.
 1. Shelley, Percy Bysshe, 1792–1822—Philosophy. 2. Shelley, Percy Bysshe, 1792–1822—Criticism and interpretation. 3. Skepticism in literature. I. Title.
PR5442.P5A2   821'.7   79–9166
ISBN 0–8032–1001–9

Manufactured in the United States of America

To Eleanor

CONTENTS

PREFACE

C. E. PULOS has demonstrated that skepticism unifies Shelley's thought.[1] After finding repeated confirmations of Pulos's position in Shelley's poems, I undertook in this study to show that skepticism is both the central theme of Shelley's poetry and the primary cause of its artistic excellence. Recent criticism has obscured the consistently skeptical tone of Shelley's work, usually by emphasizing symbolic connotation at the expense of denotative meaning. My own emphasis is mainly imagistic. But, while I have paid careful attention to Shelley's image-patterns, I have tried not to give imagery and symbol more attention than the details of the actual narratives or of the author's assertions. When, for example, in "Adonais," Shelley describes birth as an "eclipsing Curse" (l. 480) and recommends suicide (ll. 464–65), I do not conclude that these are entirely rhetorical or hyperbolic gestures, even though I am fully aware that the statements must be read in the context of an evolving symbolic pattern. If the literal meanings of Shelley's statements can be totally discounted by emphasis on their symbolic context, then the criticism of the church in Milton's "Lycidas" should, by the same logic, be equally malleable to critical revision.

But any responsible scholar would denounce such a treatment of Milton's text. The case of Shelley, however, is quite another thing. Earl R. Wasserman, the best of all Shelley critics, shows no qualms whatsoever in discounting the suicidal assertions of "Adonais," even though the assertions are phrased in the clearest, most emphatic possible terms.[2] Similarly, Donald Reiman, an excellent critic who has substantially improved the accuracy of many Shelley texts and who has given us a virtual dictionary of Shelley's symbolism, disparages scholars who assume that Shelley's literal statements always mean precisely what they say.[3]

Another pitfall I have tried to avoid is the conversion of Shelley's symbols into a set of inflexible counters, translatable at every point into dogmatic paraphrase. There is, indeed, consistency in Shelley's symbolism, but the skepticism of his poetry appears most vividly in his willingness to vary, and even reverse, the connotations of his symbols by shifting their narrative and dramatic contexts. One of the great strengths of Richard Harter Fogle's pioneering study of the imagery was his recognition of this flexibility.[4] Since Shelley's variation and redefinition of his symbols is an essential part of his skepticism, I must take issue with the reductive paraphrase that has characterized much critical analysis of his imagery. Donald Reiman's discussion of "The Triumph of Life" for example, would lead us to believe that, because Shelley's sun image has positive associations in most of his work, it will automatically retain those associations in "The Triumph of Life" regardless of how drastically its context is altered.[5] This attitude fails to take adequate account of the skepticism with which Shelley expresses his ideas. Indeed, his use of imagery can tell us as much about his skepticism as can his literal statements; in the work of Shelley, theory and practice are one.

A final word about the method I have employed. If Shelley does not assign a preface or prose passage to another, real or imagined, author, I assume the passage expresses Shelley's thought (see Wasserman's treatment of the preface to "Alastor" for the opposite practice).[6] If Shelley's poetry is not spoken by an imaginary or dramatic character, and if it is not undercut by some qualifying device (irony or humor, for example), I assume it seriously expresses the author's views.

For reading this work at widely different stages of completion, for their outstanding example as Shelley scholars, and for their criticism and encouragement, I wish to thank Milton Wilson, Ross Woodman, and Richard Harter Fogle. Milton Wilson and Ross Woodman, with their many insights into Shelley's work, were especially helpful. My whole emphasis on the *Doppelgänger* relationship reflects Ross Woodman's influence and suggestions, especially in the discussion of "Prometheus Unbound." Milton Wilson taught me much about Shelley when I was a doctoral candidate, and Richard Harter Fogle made me rethink and improve a good part of the book.

I wish also to thank the University of New Mexico Press for permission to quote selections from *Shelley's Prose or The Trumpet of a Prophecy*, edited by David Lee Clark, Copyright 1954, by the University of New Mexico Press, Albuquerque, New Mexico; and Oxford University Press for allowing me to quote from *Wordsworth: Poetical Works*, edited by Thomas Hutchinson, revised by Ernest de Selincourt (1959), and from *Shelley: Poetical Works*, edited by Thomas Hutchinson, revised by G. M. Matthews (1970); both by permission of Oxford University Press. *Shelley's "The Triumph of Life": A Critical Study* (Urbana: University of Illinois Press, 1965) is quoted by permission of Donald H. Reiman; and Yale University Press permitted me to quote from *Shelley's "Prometheus Unbound": The Text and the Drafts*, edited by L. J. Zillman, Copyright © 1968 by Yale University. The brief excerpts from Shelley's discussion of *Julie* and from his translation of *The Symposium* are taken from volumes 6 and 7 of the *Complete Works*, edited by R. Ingpen and W. E. Peck (New York: Gordian Press, 1965).

An earlier version of chapter 1 originally appeared in *Mosaic: A Journal for the Comparative Study of Literature and Ideas* 10 (July 1977): 69–84, published by the University of Manitoba Press, to whom acknowledgment is herewith made. An earlier version of chapter 6 was first published in the *Keats-Shelley Journal* 27 (1978): 69–86; and three paragraphs in chapter 5 are taken from my article "Shelley's Repudiation of Conscious Artistry," *English Studies in Canada* 1 (Spring 1975): 62–73. I thank these journals and the Association of Canadian University Teachers of English for permission to reprint this material. Five paragraphs of chapter 4 are from a paper given at a meeting of the Keats-Shelley Association of America, New York, 1978.

Finally, I would like to point out that this work has been published with the help of a grant from the Canadian Federation for the Humanities, using funds provided by the Social Sciences and Humanities Research Council of Canada.

INTRODUCTION

Percy Bysshe Shelley was in a state of almost total philosophical uncertainty throughout his career. He refused to embrace any dogma, either for the sake of social convention or for psychological comfort. What is consistent in his work is his skepticism. By demonstrating the essentially Humean cast of William Drummond's skepticism and by showing clearly the influence of Drummond on Shelley, C. E. Pulos has revealed skepticism as the one perspective from which Shelley's radicalism, immaterialism, and Platonism may be cogently reconciled and has refuted the charges of inconsistency which even sympathetic scholars have levelled against Shelley.[1] Earl R. Wasserman's ingenious studies of Shelley's ontology—especially his analysis of "Mont Blanc"—have further demonstrated the subtlety and consistency of the poet's thought.[2]

"Mont Blanc" is, indeed, the work central to the understanding of Shelley's major poetry. What the longer poems express in dramatic or narrative form is here presented in a series of metaphorical hypotheses whose intellectual implications are expounded with a subtle and rigorous logic. "Mont Blanc" makes the inscrutability of first cause the basis for the repudiation of dogmas

1

which falsely define life's origin. As symbol of the inscrutable "Power" or life-source, the mountain thus initiates a socially renovating iconoclasm:

> Thou hast a voice, great Mountain, to repeal
> Large codes of fraud and woe; not understood
> By all, but which the wise, and great, and good
> Interpret, or make felt, or deeply feel.[3]

In the framework of this ontological skepticism the poet functions as a reformer whose sole claim to moral authority is that he knows the ineffability of first cause. Drummond, acknowledging the possibility of a first cause, but insisting on the necessary inscrutability of such a cause, was, as Pulos has clearly shown, of foremost importance in shaping Shelley's skepticism. Shelley's frequent use of the term *Power* to denote first cause certainly recalls Drummond's similar use of the term: "If we consider power as the cause, by which we are ultimately to account for all effects, we must acknowledge, that it is itself a boundary, which we cannot pass—a principle, before which nothing can be placed." And further: "Power cannot be at once both the principle and the attribute of being. It cannot be both the consequence and the origin of existing substance—that by which all things were caused, and yet that, which something was necessary to cause."[4]

Drummond's view of power, however, is inconsistent with Hume's skepticism, since Hume allows no justification for assuming the existence of a first cause, no matter how inscrutable.[5] And Shelley differs from both Hume and Drummond by asserting that the imagination is an intuitive faculty whereby the existence of first cause is discerned. The apostrophe to the mountain which concludes "Mont Blanc" is not so much a celebration of imaginative insight as an admission that, without "the human mind's imaginings," the Power would remain a "vacancy" and the mountain peak could not be perceived as its symbol:

> The secret strength of things
> Which governs thought, and to the infinite dome
> Of heaven is as a law, inhabits thee!
> And what were thou, and earth, and stars, and sea,

> If to the human mind's imaginings
> Silence and solitude were vacancy?
>
> [Ll. 139–44]

Between the imaginative presentation of symbols of the life-source and the dogmatic worship of such symbols as the life-source itself falls the shadow of political and religious oppression. It is the shadow of oppression which, Shelley says in his "Essay on Christianity," distinguishes Christ's imaginative parables from the dogma of Christian prelates.[6] Shelley wrote to oppose dogma, and all his major poems, from "Alastor" to "The Triumph of Life," are both iconoclastic and skeptical.

Understanding Shelley's skepticism, one finds a new consistency and subtlety in his poetry. Critics have not understood "Alastor," for example, because they have failed to see that it is Shelley's first poetic attempt to express the skeptical ontology of "Mont Blanc" and the essay "On Life." Similarly, the widespread view that "The Revolt of Islam" is a deterministic poem results from the failure to see how it manifests the skeptical ontology of "Mont Blanc."[7] But skepticism is not an undertone in the poetry; it is the major theme. Its presence is manifested in individual poems by both statement and image, and the thematic development of the poetry as a whole is skeptical. Shelley's skepticism, while consistent, is not static. The movement from the essentially negative skepticism of "Alastor" to the later portrayals of skepticism as a socially renovating force (1816–17) reflects a significant change in Shelley's thought, as does the movement from the almost Blakean optimism of "The Revolt of Islam" to the Humean inferno of "The Triumph of Life," a poem which seems completely to deny the possibility of knowledge.

Skepticism is also the prevalent theme in Shelley's portrayal of the transcendence of phenomenal illusion. Ross Woodman begins his admirable study of Shelley with the observation that the poet's life "was dominated by two powerful forces: the drive to reform the world and the drive to transcend it." Woodman sees Shelley as reconciling these tendencies only once in the course of his career,[8] and other critics have lamented the vitiation to which these divergent aims supposedly led.[9] However, the two aspirations share a skeptical basis. If the Power is inscrutable which underlies life's thought-object interdependence, man's "spirit at enmity with nothingness and dissolution" seems equally remote from phenomenal reality.[10] This point is powerfully made when the hero of "Alastor" addresses the swan:

> "Thou hast a home,
> Beautiful bird; thou voyagest to thine home,
> Where thy sweet mate will twine her downy neck
> With thine, and welcome thy return with eyes
> Bright in the lustre of their own fond joy.
> And what am I that I should linger here,
> With voice far sweeter than thy dying notes,
> Spirit more vast than thine, frame more attuned
> To beauty, wasting these surpassing powers
> In the deaf air, to the blind earth, and heaven
> That echoes not my thoughts?"
>
> ["Alastor," ll. 280–90]

Does man possess a divine spirit or are his intimations of immortality mirages? If man's soul is indeed divine, what is the nature of its origin? To what does it return?

Shelley answers these questions with a Platonism so pervaded by skepticism that it is not, in the strict sense, Platonism at all.[11] While Plato attains knowledge of the eternal through a process of rational dialectic, Shelley disparages the reason and relies rather on imaginative intimations so fleeting and inconclusive as to call the very existence of a transcendent reality into question. Against the famous passage in "Adonais" which asserts life's impermanence before "the white radiance of Eternity," one must set Shelley's repeated emphases on man's limited capacity for transcendent perception, as well as the ambiguity of his own analogues of the eternal in "The Triumph of Life." If Shelley's work is, as Harold Bloom claims, an exploration of the limits of desire, it is his skepticism which delineates those limits in the self-destructive imagery of his poetry.[12] Shelley himself, like the West Wind, is both "destroyer and preserver," preserving his noumenal intimations in images and, at the same time, destroying faith in images through his radical iconoclasm. His poetry both asserts and demonstrates the inadequacy of its images as analogues of noumenal reality. This unique quality, the source of Shelley's peculiar artistic strength, is what this study will explore.

I begin with analyses of "Alastor," "Mont Blanc," and the "Hymn to Intellectual Beauty." "Alastor" is the most Humean of Shelley's poems, next to "The Triumph of Life." Both "Mont Blanc" and the Hymn acknowledge the reality of first cause while insisting on its ineffability and positing constructive social responses to its apprehension. But the poet of "Alastor" fails either to sustain his intimations of a transcendent realm or to translate them into constructive social action, and his life and quest are futile. His predicament clearly reflects Shelley's own metaphysical and artistic dilemma in the years between "Queen Mab" and "Mont Blanc."

"The Revolt of Islam," a poem much maligned and widely ignored, is unified thematically by what one may term "public" and "private" skepticism. Publicly, Cythna's insistence on the ineffability of first cause prompts revolutionary iconoclasm which, she prophesies in canto 9, will one day end dogmatic tyranny and usher in the millennium. Privately, the hero and heroine reflect upon the impossibility of adequately manifesting man's divine essence either in language or in life. The true home of the divine Laon and Cythna is not this world, but rather the transcendent Temple of the Spirit to which they ascend in canto 1 and at the conclusion.

Shelley's "public" skepticism extols free thought and iconoclasm as the basis for reform. This is especially important in the first two acts of "Prometheus Unbound." However, in the last two acts, Shelley's fascination with the possibility of transcendence somewhat overshadows his social concern. "The Witch of Atlas" seems to mark even more clearly the tipping of the thematic balance in Shelley's career. Here there occurs an unmistakable shift of focus from social iconoclasm to the themes of man's divinity and the transcendence of phenomenal illusion. Shelley often sees man as a divine soul imprisoned in matter. But although, as Woodman has demonstrated, the roots of this concept are to be found in Orphic Platonism, Shelley is too skeptical to be labelled an Orphic Platonist. Still, his insistence on the inadequacy of language as an expression of man's divinity is an extremely important thread in his skepticism.

For Shelley's transcendental aspiration is severely tempered—one might almost say "occluded"—by skepticism. What basis is there for belief in man's essential divinity or in a divine realm beyond this world? It is not surprising that Shelley has been placed in the camps of Christians, Platonists, Orphic Platonists, and other religious or philosophical sects, since institutionalized belief, no matter how occult, usually provides the eventual resting place for the man whose transcendental intimations, while strong enough to justify alienation from the phenomenal world, provide nothing to take this world's place.

However, on the evidence of his poetic career, it would seem that Shelley never completely succumbed to dogma of any kind, but remained, to the end, a skeptical individualist. Although Pulos has already cogently defended this position, he has not based his argument on a detailed exegesis of the major poems. At the same time, those many critics who have devoted themselves to the analysis of the major poems have ascribed to Shelley more philosophical certainty than the poetry, in my view, will support (e.g., Ellsworth Barnard's Christianity, Woodman's suicidal Orphism, Wasserman's quasi-Platonic reconciliation of transcendent and immanent divinity, especially in his exegesis of "Adonais," and Bloom's impassioned attempt to see Shelley's mythmaking as its own *raison d'être*). Shelley's skepticism precludes philosophical certainty. Since his own transcendental intuitions defy articulation, he distrusts all claims of metaphysical authority.

The more disturbing effects of this uncompromising intellectual integrity are clearly revealed in his aesthetics and in his elegy, "Adonais." If the only basis for belief in the divine is the "fading coal" of personal imaginative experience, then the most positive critical stance one can adopt is to see all truly imaginative activity—artistic, social, scientific, or religious—as having the same idiosyncratic significance.

To explain this last argument by example: all literary classics, whatever their overt themes, become for Shelley, in the absence of the philosophic or aesthetic credos on which critical distinctions are normally based, more or less imperfect reflections of the divinity he partially apprehends. As a critic, this leads him to equate Dante, Milton, Keats, Rousseau, and all his favorites as literary refractors of that indefinable "white radiance" he intimates in his inspired moments. The same individualism leads him, as poet (notably in "Adonais"), to equate all his images—water, fire, mist, stars—as analogues of the transcendent reality he personally intuits. This is the import of the apocalyptic conclusion of "Adonais": not merely that the dew of mourning is turned to the splendor of transcendence (ll. 362–63), but that the dew has possessed this anagogic significance from the first, even if only for the inspired perceiver.

To insist on such anagogic equivalence may seem intellectually perverse, but, given Shelley's skepticism, what is the alternative? To embrace one religion and discount all others? To endorse one analogue of eternity and discount all others? To do so would be to define transcendent reality in terms of earthly hierarchies. But the inscrutability of that reality precludes such definition. Still, though, the problem of articulation remains: the poet's intimations must be somehow expressed.

"The Triumph of Life" fully explores the negative implications of Shelley's poetic skepticism. If it is true to say that all great poems have the same anagogic significance, and if it is also true that transcendent reality can never be defined in any codified, communally accessible belief, then may one not as logically insist that all imaginative activity is equally ineffectual in embodying the divine? "The Triumph of Life," having made this point, goes on to express severe doubts about the very existence of a noumenal or transcendent reality. What, after all, proves the existence of such a realm? Might not the poet have misunderstood his visionary experience? If, on the surface, it seems strangely arbitrary that Shelley should not consider this possibility until 1822, there remain, as harbingers of this uncertainty, not only the emphatic portrayals of man's perceptual and imaginative weakness in "The Witch of Atlas" and the last acts of "Prometheus Unbound," but also the Humean skepticism of "Alastor," with which Shelley's mature career began. Thus "The Triumph of Life" may be said, in a sense, to bring Shelley's career full circle, leaving him in a state of total uncertainty.

Shelley's skepticism manifests itself most powerfully in his use of mirror or *Doppelgänger* (in the sense of "ghostly double") images. Accordingly, this study will pay particular attention to the development of that image-pattern. The imagery is important not only as a symbolic device within individual poems, where man's worship of his own shadow symbolizes dogmatic and false definition of transcendent reality (e.g., "The Revolt of Islam," 8.4–8), but also as a microcosm of what occurs in the corpus of Shelley's work. For example, the last two acts of "Prometheus Unbound" are, like "The Witch of Atlas," a parodic mirror of what occurs in the first two, while the last 250 lines of "Alastor" recapitulate, *without* distortion, the first 470. More significantly, whole poems come to mirror what has preceded them in Shelley's career. "The Revolt of Islam," for example, presents a journey from a cave, through water and sky, to heaven. This journey recurs in act 2 of "Prometheus Unbound," but its conceptual implications are ironically altered by the last two acts. The cave-river-air-heaven journey in "The Revolt of Islam" is itself a narrative presentation of Shelley's own perceptual journey in "Mont Blanc," and the presentation is repeated, with its positive implications rather violently reversed, in "The Witch of Atlas," "Adonais," and "The Triumph of Life." This last poem ultimately images the whole of Shelley's career in a distorting mirror, with Rousseau, aptly chosen as Shelley's own twisted *Doppelgänger*, serving as infernal presenter.

The development of the *Doppelgänger* imagery, I think, exactly parallels changes in Shelley's thought. As I read Shelley, he first intuits that a noumenal "Power" underlies phenomenal reality and that an ideal quasi-Platonic reality lies beyond this earthly realm. He then insists that both the "Power" and the "Platonic" heaven are impossible either to know or to portray and concludes that any religious or political imagery purporting to portray eternity leads only to narcissistic idolatry, to man's worship of himself in his creations. Finally, in "Adonais" and "The Triumph of Life," Shelley condemns all art, including his own, as a manifestation of idolatry. The repudiation of his own career which Shelley effects in his last poem is itself the analogue of eternity's repudiation of time. "The Triumph of Life" is a poetic representation of apocalyptic destruction which, like *The Revelation*, can only be comprehended in full when viewed from the perspective of the preceding work. In a sense, then, Shelley's career is a demonstrative exercise in self-destruction or, at least, self-repudiation.

But the repudiation has a skeptical basis. For what "The Triumph of Life" also condemns is the author's refusal to accept the limits of knowledge. In this last poem Shelley recognizes and condemns his own excessive dissatisfaction with the limits, that is to say the nature, of the human mind. To make phenomena into hypothetical symbols of ultimate reality is one thing, but to see phenomena as having value *only* as symbols of the Ultimate is to lose one's humanity in the preoccupation with transcendence. In demonstrating, recognizing, and repudiating this personal tendency, Shelley was beginning to fuse his own public and private skepticism. Publicly he opposed dogma on humanitarian grounds. Privately he regretted the mind's inability to achieve certain knowledge; to transcend phenomena. For, although Shelley was a skeptical poet, he was also very seldom at home in his skepticism. Likewise, although he was an inspired visionary, he denied the accuracy, the philosophical validity, of his own visions. He was constantly engaged in a struggle between what he wished to know and what, as a skeptic, he actually *could* know. It is, I think, to his credit that he never confused the two and that, in the end, he forswore the first for the second.

In portraying the private pursuit of transcendence as futile, "The Triumph of Life" marks the end of Shelley's quest for the absolute. By 1822 skepticism was turning his eyes from the distant things he could never see to the near things he actually could see. In its total skepticism "The Triumph of Life" is a second and greater "Alastor." And, recalling how the "Alastor" quest prepared the way for "Mont Blanc," one begins to see "The Triumph of Life" not only as palinode to the cycle of works "Alastor" began but also as prelude to a second, much greater, cycle. When one considers the theme-variation shape of the work we have, this perception of "The

Triumph of Life" seems fully justified. As a skeptic, Shelley could never come to rest in one final position, and, had he lived past 1822, would surely have re-formed his vision as long as he could write. This book is a study of the constant re-formation in the work we have, and of the skepticism it manifests.

1 EARLY MATURITY

"Alastor," "Mont Blanc," and the Hymn

The questions which Raymond D. Havens raised about "Alastor" in 1930 prompted a controversy of considerable dimensions.[1] Does the summary in Shelley's preface accurately describe the poem? Is the vision of the veiled maiden clearly related to the events which follow it? Is the poem "the off-spring of a single, dominating purpose"[2] or was Shelley really uncertain of his theme?

Havens's answers to these questions were fairly damning: he found the prefatory description of a "self-centered" hero cursed by "the furies of an irresistible passion" irreconcilable with the sterling character of the actual hero who, in the complete absence of an "evil genius" or of avenging furies, experiences a calm, passionless death.[3] Since 1930, a multitude of critics has considered the questions Havens first raised, and many have tried to refute him. But, although the defenders of "Alastor" have been legion, the dismaying diversity of their explications might seem to vindicate, rather than challenge, Havens's misgivings.[4] On the other hand, "Alastor" is so ambiguous that most of these critical hypotheses can be made to work. One can adopt one position after the other, as impartially as a chameleon, and find that, despite vast critical divergence, most of the hypotheses provide workable perspectives

11

on the vague, sprawling mass of imagery. But if "Alastor" is, as Wilson says, the *Hamlet* of Shelley criticism, its infinite suggestiveness results not from profundity and vast scope, but from artistic failure.[5] There was much truth in Havens's article. The poem is *not* fully realized and may have already prompted enough Procrustean explications to make any further discussion appear impertinent.

However, my primary purpose is not to refute other critics. Instead I wish to show how the poem's imagery and narrative anticipate the 1816 works, "Mont Blanc" and the "Hymn to Intellectual Beauty." This is an important matter, since the period between "Queen Mab" in 1812 and "Mont Blanc" in 1816 is the most crucial in Shelley's artistic and intellectual development. By tracing this development one can show that both Bloom's "imagination" and Perkins's "love" are inadequate definitions of the Power in the preface to "Alastor" and that "Alastor" is usually too ambiguous to justify any definition beyond that provided in the dictionary.[6] Still, it is an important advance after "Queen Mab."

In terms of artistic development "Queen Mab" represented a dead end for Shelley. In Ianthe's vision of the universe and of future time Shelley had exhausted the possibilities of imagination as a prognosticating power. The vision which Queen Mab reveals to Ianthe is, like the vision Michael reveals to Adam, one of preordained historical process, Providence replaced by an impersonal Necessity moving man slowly and painfully toward a secular millennium:

> "Pain and pleasure, good and evil join,
> To do the will of strong necessity,
> And life, in multitudinous shapes,
> Still pressing forward where no term can be,
> Like hungry and unresting flame
> Curls round the eternal columns of its strength."[7]

The passage suggests an infinite vista, but this historical march culminates in the millennium of the last two cantos.

Although Necessity effects its will through the actions of exemplary spirits like Ianthe, the inevitability of the process renders redundant Mab's exhortations to Ianthe, and to mankind generally:

"Oh human Spirit!" spur thee to the goal
Where virtue fixes universal peace,
And midst the ebb and flow of human things
Show somewhat stable, somewhat certain still,
A lighthouse o'er the wild of dreary waves"

[8.53–57]

Worse than this, the poem's view of imagination as a great tele-scope spanning history to the far shore of the millennium makes the poet more a soothsayer than a prophet.

What was needed for the vitalization of Shelley's art was a framework of thought in which imaginative vision would be not merely a passive pawn of Necessity but an active force, essential to the salvation and indeed the survival of civilization. This is what emerges in "Mont Blanc," where imagination does not discover the future course of history but determines it; does not perceive a spirit's visions but creates and destroys its own. Other poets might find such apocalyptic significance unnecessary, but, given Shel-ley's intense social concern, he needed this belief in the imagina-tion's power if he was to function effectively as an artist.

Out of the torments of Humean skepticism in the years between "Mab" and "Mont Blanc" Shelley forged a new confidence in imaginative power. The key to this new assurance was a concept of imagination as a faculty of intuitive reason, transcending the un-certainties of phenomenal illusion and intuiting a noumenal reality inaccessible to the senses. This is of course the essence of what one usually thinks of as the Romantic imagination. While this concept is first articulated in "Mont Blanc" and the "Hymn to Intellectual Beauty," in "Alastor" Shelley not only explores it, with a tentative skepticism, but also, for the first time, begins to work out ways of utilizing imagery for its expression.

For example, in "Alastor" he applies the term *vacancy* to metaphysical crises: the disappearance of the apparently transcen-dent dream-vision, the poet's death. I think the ambiguity of the term *vacancy* in "Alastor" results largely from Shelley's own philosophical uncertainty in 1815. At the conclusion of "Mont Blanc" the word is used again, this time precisely and with Shel-ley's own unique meaning. Significantly, the word *vacancy*, with its derivatives, does not occur in Shelley's poetry before "Alastor," despite the vastness of "Queen Mab." Of the term's twenty-six occurrences in Shelley's poetry as a whole, there are six in "Alastor," ten in "Mont Blanc," the Hymn, and "The Revolt of Islam," the three major poems which follow "Alastor" in 1816 to 1817, and two in "Prometheus Unbound."[8] I think the term has the same philosophical significance in all eighteen instances, except for two purely descriptive occurrences in "The Revolt of Islam." I say "significance" and not "meaning" because in "Alastor" the term is used ambiguously, and its full import is not clarified until 1816. It is beyond the scope of this chapter to explore the use of the word in all five poems, but I will consider its use in "Alastor" and the 1816 poems, as well as in the philosophical essay "On Life" (1819), where it has the same meaning as in "Mont Blanc."[9]

Equally intriguing is the use of the term *Power* in "Mont Blanc," the Hymn, and the preface to "Alastor." In the preface we learn that a Power "strikes the luminaries of the world," not directly, but "by awakening them to too exquisite a perception of its influences." The victims are among the best of men. They do not perceive the Power, but its influences—or at least its influences are the immediate cause of their destruction. In the poem, the hero's impulse of pursuit hovers in his mind like lightning and performs a "ministry," possibly as the agent of "that Power" mentioned in the preface. Although Shelley does not explicitly state that the "impulse" is agent of the Power, this passage *does* recall the prefatory description of the Power's workings and the passages from both poem and preface are premonitory of "Mont Blanc" and the "Hymn to Intellectual Beauty":

> Not the strong impulse hid
> In those flushed cheeks, bent eyes, and shadowy frame,
> Had yet performed its ministry: it hung
> Upon his life, as lightning in a cloud
> Gleams, hovering ere it vanish, ere the floods
> Of night close over it.
>
> [Ll. 415–20]

Let us turn, for parallels, to the 1816 poems. The Power of "Mont Blanc" "dwells apart" from mankind (l. 96) in solitudes where the

"voiceless lightning" is at home (l. 136). When the Power descends
from the mountain it assumes the Arve's likeness (l. 16), plunging
into this world "like the flame / Of lightning through the tempest"
(ll. 18–19), thus recalling the Power of the preface to "Alastor"
which strikes its victims down, probably through the lightning-like
minister described above. Similarly, in the "Hymn to Intellectual
Beauty," the Spirit of Beauty, object of the author's desire, is the
shadow of some unseen Power, but not the Power itself. In all
three poems a noumenal or at least inscrutable Power influences
man either indirectly, through the agency of a spirit or minister, or,
if directly, in the guise of phenomenal appearance.

The meaning of the term *Power* in "Mont Blanc" is clarified by the
term's imagistic and conceptual matrix. Wasserman's study of
"Mont Blanc" has shown how Shelley's imagery portrays the
interdependence of thought and its objects in maintaining existence. If, as Shelley says, "nothing exists but as it is perceived,"[10]
while, at the same time, "we can think of nothing which we have
not perceived,"[11] then thought and its objects are interdependent
in maintaining life. Behind the phenomenal warp and woof of
thought and its objects lies a noumenal "Power" ("Mont Blanc," l.
127), symbolized in "Mont Blanc" by the mountain's inaccessible
peak.

Repeatedly in "Mont Blanc" we are presented with phenomenal
process which produces an object of perception, the process symbolizing the interweaving of thought and its objects and the re-
sulting object of perception symbolizing life. Always behind this
phenomenal interdependence is an inscrutable third element
which symbolizes the Power. This image-pattern is illustrated very
well in "Mont Blanc," in the opening of the second section. The
"thus" which begins this passage refers to the description of
thought-object interdependence in the first section:

> Thus thou, Ravine of Arve—dark, deep Ravine—
> Thou many-coloured, many voiced vale,
> Over whose pines, and crags, and caverns sail
> Fast cloud-shadows and sunbeams: awful scene,
> Where Power in likeness of the Arve comes down
> From the ice-gulfs that gird his secret throne,

Bursting through these dark mountains like the flame
Of lightning through the tempest;—thou dost lie,
Thy giant brood of pines around thee clinging,
Children of elder time, in whose devotion
The chainless winds still come and ever came
To drink their odours, and their mighty swinging
To hear—an old and solemn harmony;
Thine earthly rainbows stretched across the sweep
Of the aethereal waterfall, whose veil
Robes some unsculptured image; the strange sleep
Which when the voices of the desert fail
Wraps all in its own deep eternity.

[Ll. 12–29]

The Ravine of Arve is like the "mind" of the first eleven lines: it amplifies the Arve's descent to produce an echoing roar in its "many voiced vale," just as the mind modifies sense-objects into phenomenal appearances and abstractions; into what we know as existence. As the ravine's "brood," the pines are an extension of the ravine and, just as the ravine amplifies the river's descent, so the swinging of the pines harmonizes with the song of the winds, while the rainbow created by the sun's light and the river's mist veils some undefined third element (l. 27).

The descent of the Power is the ultimate cause of the "Mont Blanc" universe—it is responsible for the pines, the rainbow mist, the hollowing of the ravine itself. However, only its "likeness" can be known; one never perceives it directly but only intuits it as the noumenal silence behind phenomenal sound ("the strange sleep / Which when the voices of the desert fail / Wraps all in its own deep eternity"), as the shapeless force behind phenomenal imagery ("some unsculptured image"). Yet precisely because the Power is inscrutable, the intuition of its existence frees one from dogmatic explanations of life's origin and meaning. The doubt it teaches is a distrust of religious dogma; the faith an awareness that, beyond the natural world, there is another reality. This awareness precludes man's reconciliation with nature's cyclic flux:

The wilderness has a mysterious tongue
Which teaches awful doubt, or faith so mild,

So solemn, so serene, that man may be,
But for such faith, with nature reconciled. [12]

[Ll. 76-79]

This articulate nature, through which man intuits the Power's existence, is to be contrasted with the "vacancy" nature presents to man when he is not imaginatively inspired (ll. 142-44). Because he can conceive of a realm beyond nature, the man who intuits the Power will never find spiritual fulfillment in the natural world. In this connection, it is useful to contrast the "Alastor" poet's youthful communion with nature ("He would linger long / In lonesome vales, making the wild *his home*" [ll. 98-99, my italics]) with the alienation from the natural world he experiences after grasping the occult secrets mentioned in line 128 and experiencing the vision of the veiled maiden (see his apostrophe to the swan, ll. 280-90). This drastic change suggests that the hero's perception of the secrets, as well perhaps as his vision of the maiden, involves momentary transcendence of the natural world. Such transcendence is a definite part of the intuition "Mont Blanc" describes.

If the Power, in "Mont Blanc," enters this world only in the guise of natural phenomena, the Power of the "Hymn to Intellectual Beauty" is similarly known only through its analogues. These analogues differ from those in "Mont Blanc," however, being predominantly "beautiful" rather than sublime. Instead of mighty ravine and crashing rapids, we have in this poem moonbeams and pines (l. 5), clouds in starlight (l. 9), and "sympathies" in lovers' eyes (ll. 42-43). The reference to the sunlight weaving rainbows over a mountain river (ll. 18-19), though, is an unmistakable allusion to the phenomenal interdependence of "Mont Blanc" and suggests that, in the Hymn, Shelley is considering the Power of "Mont Blanc" primarily as it is intuited through imaginative perception of the beautiful. Shelley departs from this theme only in the Gothic description of stanza 5, which constitutes something of a lapse.

Man's capacity for imaginative perception of the beautiful is personified in the Hymn as the Spirit of Beauty, whose visitations portray imaginative inspiration both in their evanescence [13] and in their capacity to modify perception by a divine inner light: [14]

> Spirit of BEAUTY, that dost consecrate
> With thine own hues all thou dost shine upon
> Of human thought or form,—where art thou gone?
> Why dost thou pass away and leave our state,
> This dim vast vale of tears, vacant and desolate?
>
> [Ll. 13–17]

While imaginative inspiration makes possible intuition of the unseen Power underlying perception, the loss of imagination leaves
the environment "vacant." Without imaginative vision, the environment cannot give intimations of the life-source. This point is
also made in Shelley's apostrophe to Mont Blanc:

> And what were thou, and earth, and stars, and sea,
> If to the human mind's imaginings
> Silence and solitude were vacancy?
>
> [Ll. 142–44]

If the human mind did not image the Power as mountain, star, or
whatever, the Power would remain a "vacancy" to man. Accordingly, the mountain and the entire physical environment would
lose their wonder as veils of the inscrutable life-source. The veil of
life would become, as in the second stanza of the Hymn, a "dim
vast vale of tears."

But any objects of perception which symbolize the life-source
must remain mere metaphors for the unknown. If one accepts
metaphorical images of the Power as the Power itself, one will
succumb to superstition and idolatry. Poets and sages cannot
accurately describe ultimate reality:

> The names of God and ghosts and Heaven,
> Remain the records of their vain endeavour,
> Frail spells—whose uttered charm might not avail to sever,
> From all we hear and all we see,
> Doubt, chance, and mutability
> Thy light alone—like mist o'er mountains driven,
> Or music by the night-wind sent
> Through strings of some still instrument,
> Or moonlight on a midnight stream,
> Gives grace and truth to life's unquiet dream.
>
> [Ll. 27–36]

The reference to the wind-harp recalls the similar reference in the
invocation of "Alastor" (ll. 41–49), where the author calls upon the

breath of Nature to flow over him in imaginative inspiration, even as it flows over the poet of the narrative, who is presented as a living aeolian lyre ("A fragile lute, on whose harmonious strings / The breath of heaven did wander" [ll. 667–68]).[15] The rest of the passage explains the radical function which imagination performs when it gives intuition of the inscrutable life-source.

This function is to prompt, in both the individual and his society, a repudiation of dogma. Sages make records of their "vain endeavour" to know ultimate reality. In the hands of lesser men, these records become religious dogma ("God and ghosts and Heaven") and are "uttered" as "charms"; uttered with certainty, even while we see the evidence of "chance" and "mutability" all around us. Imaginative intuition of the Power, however, prompts us to a realization that the life-source is inscrutable. This realization liberates men ("Gives grace and truth to life's unquiet dream"); it ends our passive slavery to dogmatic authority. Accordingly, in stanza 6 of the Hymn, Shelley expresses his hope that the Spirit of Beauty, agent of intuition, may one day free the world entirely from the salvery of religious and political dogma:

> Never joy illumed my brow
> Unlinked with hope that thou wouldst free
> This world from its dark slavery.
>
> [Ll. 68–70]

Similarly, in "Mont Blanc," the mountain's function as symbol of the inscrutable life-source renders it, metaphorically, a destroyer of dogmatic religious and political codes. Those who intuit the life-source also serve as its ministers in society. Intuition of the Power thus initiates a mission to promote social reform:

> Thou hast a voice, great Mountain, to repeal
> Large codes of fraud and woe; not understood
> By all, but which the wise, and great, and good
> Interpret, or make felt, or deeply feel.
>
> [Ll. 80–83]

"Mont Blanc" and the Hymn emphasize the necessity for both imaginative symbol making and imaginative iconoclasm which will prevent symbols of the unknowable Power from being taken as realities. Shelley's empirical skepticism dictates that the poet must be at once image maker and image breaker, creator and destroyer, or both he and his society are in peril.

This conception of the poet's role is definitely foreshadowed in the invocation of "Alastor" when the narrator (Shelley)[16] tells the "Great Parent" (Spirit of Nature as Wasserman rightly observes):[17]

> I have made my bed
> In charnels and on coffins, where black death
> Keeps record of the trophies won from thee,
> Hoping to still these obstinate questionings
> Of thee and thine, by forcing some lone ghost,
> Thy messenger, to render up the tale
> Of what we are.
>
> [Ll. 23–29]

The Immortality Ode, echoed here, was frequently before Shelley in the years 1815 to 1816 and undoubtedly contributed to his own obstinate questionings in the 1819 essay "On Life." The phrase, "the tale / Of what we are," Wordsworthian in its recognition of the wonder and mystery of the immediate, anticipates Shelley's question in the essay "On Life": "What are we?"[18] The essay answers this question only by negatives. The source of our existence, we are told, cannot in any way resemble mind. In seeking "the tale / Of what we are," the author of the invocation is seeking knowledge of our destiny and origin.

The quoted passage clearly parallels the fifth stanza of the "Hymn to Intellectual Beauty," in which Shelley describes his earliest attempts to discover what lies beyond mortal life:

> While yet a boy I sought for ghosts, and sped
> Through many a listening chamber, cave and ruin,
> And starlight wood, with fearful steps pursuing
> Hopes of high talk with the departed dead.
> I called on poisonous names with which our youth is fed;
> I was not heard—I saw them not—
> When musing deeply on the lot
> Of life . . .
> . . . .
> Sudden, thy shadow fell on me;
> I shrieked, and clasped my hands in ecstasy!
>
> [Ll. 49–60]

In both "Alastor" and the Hymn, Shelley used Gothic imagery ("in charnels and on coffins" [l. 24]) to portray his search for forbidden knowledge. While in the Hymn this knowledge is awareness of the Power, "Alastor" leaves the exact nature of the knowledge undefined. Nevertheless, it is clear that the imagery of "Alastor" strongly anticipates that of the two later poems.

Like the Shelley of the invocation, the "Alastor" poet also seeks occult knowledge. When the poet leaves his alienated home (ll. 76–77), he too is pursuing an awareness his family and society cannot give. Although his infancy is nurtured by visions and dreams (l. 67), this imaginative activity does not enable the poet to attain occult knowledge, just as the author's supernatural intimations arouse a desire for spiritual insight these visions only adumbrate:

> and, though ne'er yet
> Thou hast unveil'd thy inmost sanctuary,
> Enough from incommunicable dream,
> And twilight phantasms . . .
> Has shone within me, that . . .
> . . . .
> I wait thy breath, Great Parent.
>
> [Ll. 39–45]

The author awaits the breath of imaginative inspiration, hoping that through imaginative vision he may penetrate Nature's "inmost sanctuary." Wasserman argues that, because the speaker of the invocation addresses his prayer to Nature, the knowledge he seeks cannot transcend the natural world. "Mont Blanc," however, would seem to refute this claim. It is, after all, through his own imaginative perception of the natural scene in the Vale of Chamouni that Shelley intuits the Power underlying Nature. This Power could well be described as Nature's "inmost sanctuary" (l. 40).

In the face of this parallel, Wasserman's insistence on the philosophical opposition of narrator and hero seems suspect.[19] It is true, as Wasserman points out, that the narrator's sorrow at the hero's death suggests a disbelief in transcendence (ll. 649–720), but, since the hero himself is uncertain whether his death will bring transcendence or extinction (ll. 290–95), there is no real opposition here. Moreover, the narrator himself expresses uncertainty on this point (ll. 427–30).

Presumably, though—and this tends to discredit Wasserman as well—the "strange truths" which the poet pursues reveal what the narrator also wishes to learn. Whether or not these truths may be equated with the inscrutable Power of "Mont Blanc" the poet's perception of them strongly foreshadows Shelley's transcendent intuition in the later poem.

The geography of the poet's earliest wanderings suggests that the object of his quest is knowledge of life's source. The poet, in the early stages of his travels, reveals an intense interest in those ancient civilizations whose rise marked the beginnings of recorded history. By tracing history back to its beginnings one might conceivably discover some clue to the origin of human life:

> His wandering step
> Obedient to high thoughts, has visited
> The awful ruins of the days of old.
>
> [Ll. 107–9]

The following passage indicates that the poet did in fact gain intuition of life's source by studying the past:

> He lingered, poring on memorials
> Of the world's youth, through the long burning day
> Gazed on those speechless shapes, nor, when the moon
> Filled the mysterious halls with floating shades
> Suspended he that task, but ever gazed
> And gazed, till meaning on his vacant mind
> Flashed like strong inspiration, and he saw
> The thrilling secrets of the birth of time.
>
> [Ll. 121–28]

The phrase, "the thrilling secrets of the birth of time," means "the secrets of *how time was born*"; i.e., the secrets of the source of mortal existence.[20] This is clear from both parallels and contrasts between this passage and passages of "Mont Blanc" and the Hymn which describe intuition of the Power or life-source.

The poet who "gazed and gazed" on the ancient ruins is the prototype of the author of the invocation who gazes on Nature's mysteries (ll. 22–23). The author has made his bed "in charnels and on coffins" just as the poet studies the graves of dead civilizations by night. The poet's mind is "vacant" when he sees the secrets. In the terms of the 1816 poems, vacancy is what man confronts when, without imagination, he seeks to discover the source of his own thought. In the last lines of "Mont Blanc" Shelley suggests that the Power would remain a "vacancy" if man did not intuit it in his solitude. In itself this does not prove that the "Alastor" poet's vacancy is ignorance of the life-source, but the parallel with "Mont Blanc" goes farther than this. We are told that the secrets come to the poet "like strong inspiration" and "flash" upon his mind. The diction indicates that they come to the poet as an imaginative intuition—and it is through "the human mind's imaginings" ("Mont Blanc," l. 141) that the Power is intuited and imaged.

The consequences of the poet's perception present an instructive contrast with "Mont Blanc" and the Hymn. As Shelley shows in the "Hymn to Intellectual Beauty," intuition of the inscrutable Power carries with it the responsibility of promoting social reform. This promotion of reform is to be effected through the repudiation of those dogmatic explanations of existence which are the basis for religious and political tyranny. In the essay "On Life" Shelley asserts that "it is the duty of the reformer in political and ethical questions to leave [behind him] a vacancy."[21] Here, as in "Mont Blanc," the term *vacancy* denotes both ignorance of life's source and the failure of one's environment to intimate noumenal reality. Such vacancy, though intellectually dissatisfying, is better than enslavement to dogmatic illusion. The reformer will create this vacancy in the place once occupied by the king, Jehovah, or whatever dogmatic authority enslaves mankind. In stanza 7 of the "Hymn to Intellectual Beauty," Shelley reflects that his imaginative intuition of the Power has not only enabled him to love mankind but has *bound* him to do so (ll. 83–84). In "Mont Blanc," the mountain, as symbol of the Power, is a potential agent of social change (ll. 80–81), at least when perceived by the Power's imaginative ministers (l. 83).

But the poet's spurning of the Arab maiden immediately after he attains his imaginative intuition reveals him as a self-centered visionary, totally indifferent to his fellows. The incident is not presented as a major event in the narrative, but in an almost cursory manner, as if Shelley were uncertain of its significance. However, its presence immediately after the occult perception shows that here Shelley is beginning to trace the connection between imaginative insight and social responsibility which becomes a major theme in "Mont Blanc" and the Hymn. There is a similar connection between insight and responsibility in "Queen Mab" where the Fairy Queen exhorts Ianthe to be a lighthouse to her society. But the possibility that Ianthe might fail in this obligation is never raised; she is too ideal a being for that. The "Alastor" poet, however, does not translate his insight into human concern. "Mont Blanc" and the Hymn are both emphatic on the necessity to do so. By 1816 Shelley had become intensely aware that even the inspired seer might fail his vision.

Certainly the poet's treatment of the Arab maiden is reprehensible. Instead of showing concern for her obvious unhappiness, the poet is oblivious to the maiden, as he is to all human beings (ll. 129–39). The poet does not consciously set out to hurt the Arab maiden, but he does so nevertheless, as her haggard appearance shows ("wildered, and wan" [l. 139]). The similarity of the poet's fate to the Arab maiden's (he is wasted by unfulfilled desire) suggests that his imaginative vision of the veiled maiden is indeed a nemesis which comes to him as a result of his "self-centered seclusion." It is, moreover, a nemesis which he brings upon himself. Like the astronomer in Samuel Johnson's "The History of Rasselas," he is driven to delusion by the isolation he has imposed upon himself. [22]

Before experiencing his disastrous vision, however, the poet enjoys a brief period of tranquillity. The intuition among the ruined temples leaves the poet, as the preface tells us, "joyous." The poem bears out Shelley's prose statement ("The poet wandering on, through Arabie / . . . In joy and exultation held his way" [ll. 140–44]). The poet is joyful because, in the words of the preface, the object intuited by his imagination is "infinite" and "unmeasured." His intuition has given him momentary access to occult knowledge, but his secret knowledge in no way alters his solitary way of life or his indifference to others. Soon, however, "the spirit of sweet human love" (l. 203) sends to the poet the vision of the veiled maid. The spirit is the poet's own need for love, a need he fails to acknowledge before the maiden's appearance. The poet's absorption in the vision of the veiled maid is so intense that it erases all other concerns from his mind. Accordingly, as the dream vision fades, the poet is left with only the "vacancy" of his original ignorance:

> His wan eyes
> Gaze on the empty scene as vacantly
> As ocean's moon looks on the moon in heaven.
>
> [Ll. 200–2]

Here the "vacancy" is both the poet's inability to penetrate phenomenal appearance and the failure of the natural environment—ocean and moon—to present more than phenomenal illusion.

If one views the dream vision in this way, the second paragraph of the preface makes at least partial sense. There we learn that the poet perished because he was awakened "to too exquisite a perception" of the "influences" of "that Power which strikes the luminaries of the world." To illustrate the close affinity between "Alastor" and "Mont Blanc," let us assume for a moment that the Power of the preface to "Alastor" is the inscrutable life-source of the later poem, and that, in the thrilling secrets of the birth of time, the poet's imagination gained intuition of the Power. The sentence from the preface is ambiguous, but the "influences" of the Power could well involve the "spirit of . . . human love" which should ideally prompt man to love his fellows as a result of his intuition, but which, in the poet's case, brings disaster. The preface emphasizes that "among those who attempt to exist without human sympathy, the pure and tenderhearted perish through the intensity and passion of their search after its communities, when the *vacancy* of their spirit suddenly makes itself felt" (my italics). The poet is not conscious of his need for human sympathy when he spurns the Arab maiden, but his vision of the veiled maiden makes him realize his own isolation. When the vision vanishes, the vacancy of his spirit indeed "makes itself felt" (ll. 189–91, 195–96, 200–2; cf. "Mont Blanc," ll. 142–44, Hymn, ll. 13–17) in his inability to penetrate nature's veil. "Does the bright arch of rainbow clouds, / And pendent mountains seen in the calm lake, / Lead only to a black and watery depth?" (ll. 213–15). Does nature veil a transcendent realm or is the natural world all there is? Bereft of imaginative insight, the poet cannot know.

At this point, "Alastor" illustrates another important step in Shelley's artistic growth. As he matures, the suspense of his poetry inheres increasingly in symbolic description rather than narrative development. In "Queen Mab" our ignorance of history's resolution is not fully relieved until the last two cantos, while in "Prometheus Unbound" the battle against oppression is won in the first act, where Prometheus reveals his forgiveness of Jupiter and the inevitability of the tyrant's fall. What is of interest in the remainder of the poem is Shelley's exploration of the nature and consequences of the fall itself. Similarly, in "Alastor," less than a third of the poem has passed when the dream-vision concludes, but the remaining lines do not resolve the problem of the vision; rather they attempt, unsuccessfully perhaps, a symbolic exploration of its implications. The long stretches of natural description are perplexing and ambiguous, but they are also a step toward one central achievement, not only of Shelley's poetry, but of Romantic poetry generally; namely, the detailed symbolic portrayal of a private ontology.

The last quotation illustrates how Shelley makes the imagery of this poem symbolize the hero's metaphysical dilemma, a development which intensifies as the poem proceeds. In the last 250 lines of "Alastor" all the preceding events are symbolically recapitulated. Whatever the purpose of this recapitulation, it shows Shelley using natural images to portray ideas at a length and consistency unprecedented in his work and strongly premonitory of the total fusion of idea and image in "Mont Blanc."

The image of lines 472 to 473 ("the human heart, / Gazing in dreams over the gloomy grave") recalls the author of the invocation ("My heart ever gazes on the depth / Of [Nature's] deep mysteries" [ll. 22–23]) as well as the poet in the early stages of his quest, who, while exploring the graves of earliest civilization, "ever gazed / And gazed, till meaning on his vacant mind / Flashed like strong inspiration" (ll. 125–27). In these passages both author and poet were pursuing (and, in the poet's case, attaining) intuition of those secrets which would, in "Mont Blanc," become the Power. In lines 472 to 473, then, the "Alastor" poet would appear to be again approaching, unintentionally perhaps, this occult knowledge. These lines begin a symbolic recapitulation of the entire action of the poem up to this point.

This recapitulation is effected through the imagery employed from line 469 to line 601. For example: the fountain of the well on which the poet gazes in line 473 comes from "secret springs" (l. 478). This reference anticipates "Mont Blanc," where human perception is described in line 4 as coming from "secret springs," the secret source of perception which is the Power. In gazing on the well with its submerged springs the poet is symbolically approaching perception of the occult secrets he originally sought. However, while he attempts to perceive the springs of the well, the poet's attention is suddenly distracted by the Spirit which seems to stand beside him (ll. 479–92). This Spirit is in fact only his memory of the veiled maiden, a product of his troubled mind ("two starry eyes, hung in the gloom of thought" [l. 490]). However, the Spirit's eyes cause him to turn from the secret springs in eager pursuit (ll. 493–94). From here to line 601 the natural imagery gives us a symbolic portrayal of an extremely accelerated life cycle,[23] just as in lines 248 to 254 it becomes evident that the poet's physical decay is hastening his movement toward the grave ("His limbs were lean; his scattered hair / Sered by the autumn of strange suffering / Sung dirges in the wind" [ll. 248–50]). Thus, there occurs a microcosmic repetition of the narrative's over-all pattern.

A scrutiny of the reference to "secret springs" from the perspective of "Mont Blanc" is clearly justified by the poet's soliloquy of lines 502 to 514. In this soliloquy the poet approaches the metaphysical perspective of "Mont Blanc":

"O stream!
Whose source is inaccessibly profound,

Whither do thy mysterious waters tend?
Thou imagest my life. Thy darksome stillness,
Thy dazzling waves, thy loud and hollow gulfs,
Thy searchless fountain, and invisible course
Have each their type in me: and the wide sky,
And measureless ocean may declare as soon
What oozy cavern or what wandering cloud
Contains thy waters, as the universe
Tell where these living thoughts reside, when stretched
Upon thy flowers my bloodless limbs shall waste
I' the passing wind!"

Compare with this the opening lines of "Mont Blanc":

The everlasting universe of things
Flows through the mind, and rolls its rapid waves,
Now dark—now glittering—now reflecting gloom—
Now lending splendour, where from secret springs
The source of human thought its tribute brings
Of waters.

[Ll. 1–6]

The stream of the first passage, like the universe in the second passage, has an inaccessible source ("Alastor," l. 503; "Mont Blanc," l. 97). In "Mont Blanc" the "darksome," "dazzling" course of the "Alastor" stream becomes the "dark" and "glittering" passage of impressions through the collective mind. While the poet of "Alastor" does not perceive the existential interdependence of mind and stream, he nevertheless approaches this awareness in his realization that the flow of the stream typifies the flow of his perceptions. Ocean and sky are macrocosm to the stream in the same way that "the universe" is macrocosm to the poet's "living thoughts." This is much more than a conventional "stream-of-life" image. The elements of "Mont Blanc" are so vividly present that, had the poet, or Shelley, gazed a moment longer, the obscurity of "Alastor" would surely have been dispelled, its universe becoming "the everlasting universe of things," and the "secret springs" "the source of human thought." But, unlike the Shelley of "Mont Blanc," the poet has no concept of a collective consciousness which sustains and is sustained by the universe; he cannot regard the universe as "everlasting." In his prose, Shelley does not give full expression to the One Mind concept until the essay "On Life" (1819). Were it not for its late date, that essay could well be seen as a bridge between the comparatively vague empirical skepticism of "Alastor" and the more systematic and universal expression of that skepticism in "Mont Blanc." As it is, the essay shows that the skepticism of "Mont Blanc" did not essentially alter over the next three years and thereby further demonstrates the consistency of Shelley's thought and art.

This reading explains a good deal of the ambiguity of "Alastor." In this poem Shelley employed natural imagery at bewildering length to symbolize the mind's relation to both the noumenal and phenomenal worlds. But his failure to define the nature of that relationship left the implications of his symbols open to question. Are the "thrilling secrets" knowledge of a transcendent heaven, of a god, of God, of a first mover? Is the veiled maiden real or illusory? The critical controversy over the poem is understandable, because these questions cannot be answered in the terms which the poem provides. The symbolic import of the imagery, while clear in the wind-harp and rainbow motifs and in the poet's address to the stream, is more often left undefined. To that extent, "Alastor" is a failure.

However, one sees here Shelley's first attempt to use rivers, rainbows, and other natural phenomena as symbols of a complex metaphysical dilemma. He employs similar imagery in "Queen Mab," but never with the sustained detail that occurs in the poet's address to the stream and seldom with such general reluctance to specify explicitly the tenor of the comparison. This leads to some obscurity in "Alastor," but bears fruit in the subtle and thoroughly consistent symbolism of "Mont Blanc."

The following example from "Queen Mab" is typical of Shelley's earliest procedure:

> "Death is a gate of dreariness and gloom,
> That leads to azure isles and beaming skies
> And happy regions of eternal hope."
>
> [9.161–63]

To move from such self-explicating metaphors to "Mont Blanc," where the correspondence between natural phenomena and the view of reality they symbolize is sustained throughout the poem, usually implicitly, is like moving from Beethoven's early sonata movements to the opening of the *Eroica*; in short, it is a step into the mainstream of Romantic art. In "Alastor," whatever its deficiencies, one not only sees Shelley making this difficult transition, but also derives considerable insight into his state of mind in late 1815. Skeptical, tentatively experimenting in both thought and poetry, but reluctant as yet to commit himself to a new intellectual position, Shelley had far outgrown the naïve didacticism of "Queen Mab." The uneasy amalgamation of materialism and Platonism in "Queen Mab" was clearly unsatisfactory, but what was to take its place?[24] In "Alastor," Shelley hovers at the verge of his intellectual and artistic maturity, developing the terms and symbols that "Mont Blanc" and the Hymn would define and clarify and, typically, grasping the poetic shape of his idea before grasping the idea itself.

2   DESCENT TO HEAVEN

"The Revolt of Islam"

SHELLEY modifies the archetypes of transcendent ascent and of the descent for knowledge to make them portray his skepticism. Rather than progressing from ignorance to illumination, Shelley's characters in purgatory tend to travel toward ignorance. In this, Shelley's work contrasts sharply with that of other Romantics.

Wordsworth's childhood lake-journey, a descent into the wilderness, gives him a terrifying hint of noumenal reality:

> No familiar shapes
> Remained, no pleasant images of trees,
> Of sea or sky, no colours of green fields;
> But huge and mighty forms, that do not live
> Like living men, moved slowly through the mind
> By day, and were a trouble to my dreams.
> [*The Prelude* (1850), ll. 395–400]

But by the time Wordsworth has ascended Snowdon in book 14 of *The Prelude* the hint has become certainty, and the awe has been balanced by understanding:

> A mind sustained
> By recognitions of transcendent power,
> In sense conducting to ideal form,

31

In soul of more than mortal privilege
. . . .
Had Nature shadowed there, by putting forth,
'Mid circumstances awful and sublime,
That mutual domination which she loves
To exert upon the face of outward things.

[Ll. 74-82]

In "Prometheus Unbound," Asia's descent to the cave of Demogorgon only reinforces her ignorance of first causes:

If the abysm
Could vomit forth its secrets:—but a voice
Is wanting, the deep truth is imageless;
For what would it avail to bid thee gaze
On the revolving world? What to bid speak
Fate, Time, Occasion, Chance and Change? To these
All things are subject but eternal Love.[1]

"Eternal Love" is what Asia opposes to metaphysical uncertainty. But if love is not subject to historical vicissitude, the denouement of the drama reveals that neither does love control it. Skepticism and love are preferable to Jupiter's dogmatism and hatred and will defeat them every time, as the immediate ascent (2.4.150-74) of both Asia and Demogorgon reveals, but there is no conclusive proof that the ensuing social order is based on any kind of metaphysical certainty, nor that it will survive:

Gentleness, Virtue, Wisdom, and Endurance,
These are the seals of that most firm assurance
Which bars the pit over Destruction's strength;
And if, with infirm hand, Eternity,
Mother of many acts and hours, should free
The serpent that would clasp her with his length;
These are the spells by which to reassume
An empire o'er the disentangled doom.

[4.562-69, my italics]

We are also reminded that the transcendence of Prometheus and Asia is beyond the reach of man:

We will sit and talk of time and change,
As the world ebbs and flows, ourselves unchanged.
What can hide man from Mutability?

[3.3.23-25]

This is the logical result of the earlier revelation that Asia's "eternal Love," like the love of the Witch of Atlas, surpasses man's erotic capacity. Because Asia's love is stronger than man's her initial expression of it causes her grief. There is no mortal creature who can reciprocate it fully:

> Love, like the atmosphere
> Of the sun's fire filling the living world,
> Burst from thee, and illumined earth and heaven
> And the deep ocean and the sunless caves,
> And all that dwells within them; till grief cast
> Eclipse upon the soul from which it came.
>
> [2.5.26–31]

In this Asia resembles the immortal Witch of Atlas, who must reject mortal lovers, though it causes her grief to do so:

> "I cannot die as ye must—over me
> Your leaves shall glance—the streams in which ye dwell
> Shall be my paths henceforth, and so—farewell!"
> She spoke and wept.
>
> [Ll. 238–41]

This is surely the import of the dying fall in the Life of Life lyric, as well—a mortal hymn of praise to immortal Asia:

> Lamp of Earth! where'er thou movest
> Its dim shapes are clad with brightness
> And the souls of whom thou lovest
> Walk upon the winds with lightness
> Till they fail, as I am failing,
> Dizzy, lost, yet unbewailing!
>
> [2.5.66–71]

Asia's grief turns to joy when she realizes that her own immortal love will be reciprocated by that of the immortal Prometheus (2.5.44–47), but this marriage of the giants still leaves man at the mercy of his own vacillations (3.3.23–25; 3.4.193–204; 4.562–69). There is thus a characteristic refusal here to accommodate the ascent and descent archetypes to their traditional meanings, as well as a reluctance to specify the nature of the transcendent vision.

Thus "Prometheus Unbound" achieves that apocalyptic skepticism unique to Shelley, often characterized as his "urbanity."[2]

Shelley's interest in the archetypes of ascent and descent is apparent from the beginning of his career. In "Queen Mab," Ianthe ascends through the stars, sees all time and space spread out beneath her, suffers through visions of historical depravity, and finally receives the assurance that human suffering will usher in the millennium. This is Shelley's version of the *felix culpa* theme and, whatever its artistic shortcomings, it shares with *Paradise Lost* an epic assurance in the absolute validity of its vision. Skepticism begins in "Alastor," where the true nature of the hero's dream-vision is never satisfactorily explained. It continues in "Mont Blanc" and the "Hymn to Intellectual Beauty," where poetic vision comes, not from an omniscient and articulate fairy queen, but from the evanescent visitations of an inscrutable and decidedly inhuman "Power." In the shadowy figure of Demogorgon, "Prometheus Unbound" dramatically portrays this noumenal force, whose striking similarity to Milton's Death admirably captures the menace of the unknown. Moreover, "Prometheus Unbound," unlike "Queen Mab," distinguishes sublunar time from the eternity of the immortals, thereby lending ironic distance to its portrayal of Asia's transcendence.

Shelley's prose provides a philosophical underpinning for his poetic portrayals of the noumenal Power. If, as Shelley believed by 1816, "nothing exists but as it is perceived,"[3] while, at the same time, "we can think of nothing which we have not perceived,"[4] then thought and sense objects are interactive in weaving a phenomenal reality which veils life's underlying cause. Shelley is as emphatic in his prose as in his poetry on the inscrutability of this cause or Power: "What is the cause of life? . . . What agencies distinct from life . . . act upon life? . . . That the basis of all things cannot be . . . mind is sufficiently evident. Mind . . . cannot create, it can only perceive. . . . It is infinitely improbable that the cause of mind, that is, of existence, is similar to mind."[5] The poetic analogue of this mystery is the silence of Demogorgon before Asia's urgent questions or the inscrutability of Mont Blanc's icy peak.

Skepticism is also emphasized in the companion poem to "Mont Blanc," the "Hymn to Intellectual Beauty," where the noumenal presence intuited by the imagination is described only as "some unseen Power" (l. 1) and where the Spirit of Beauty which informs man's noumenal intimations has an inexplicable evanescence:

> Spirit of BEAUTY, that dost consecrate
> With thine own hues all thou dost shine upon
> Of human thought or form,—where art thou gone?
> Why dost thou pass away and leave our state,
> This dim vast vale of tears, vacant and desolate?
>
> [Ll. 13–17]

Vacancy here is our total ignorance of a noumenal reality which, without the metaphors created by imagination, would remain merely a vast question mark:

> And what were thou, and earth, and stars, and sea,
> If to the human mind's imaginings
> Silence and solitude were vacancy?
>
> ["Mont Blanc," ll. 142–44]

But imaginative metaphors for the noumenal must be regarded skeptically; dogma results from the literal-minded worship of metaphorical images (Jehovah, king). According to Shelley, no one has ever satisfactorily explained the nature of noumenal reality, nor accounted for the evanescence of its imaginative intimations:

> No voice from some sublimer world hath ever
> To sage or poet these responses given—
> Therefore the name of God and ghosts and Heaven,
> Remain the records of their vain endeavour.
>
> [Hymn, ll. 25–28]

Thus Shelley's dedication to the Spirit of Beauty is also an opposition to the "dark slavery" of dogmatic oppression:

> I vowed that I would dedicate my powers
> To thee and thine . . .
> . . . .
>   . . . Never joy illumed my brow
> Unlinked with hope that thou wouldst free
> This world from its dark slavery.
>
> [Hymn, ll. 61–70]

The literal verbal echoes of the Hymn in the dedication of "The Revolt of Islam" (cf. Hymn, 5, Dedication, 4) and in the description of Cythna's childhood recall this messianic iconoclasm.

"The Revolt of Islam" utilizes imagery of ascent and descent as the unifying motif in a complex poetic narrative. Like Ianthe in "Queen Mab," Laon and Cythna in "The Revolt of Islam" ascend into a heaven from which they survey world history. Yet this heaven differs significantly from the heaven of "Queen Mab": Shelley has taken pains to emphasize its transcendence; to emphasize that it represents a state of being which poetic metaphor can never adequately portray. Hence the ascent pattern of "Queen Mab" has been redefined in the light of Shelley's skepticism. Similarly, the descent here is not a physical descent but a descent into the cave of the mind. What we, as readers, learn in that cave is that the source of perception is unknowable. The parallel with "Mont Blanc" is obvious. "The Revolt of Islam" takes the cave and descent images of the earlier poem ("Mont Blanc," ll. 41–48) and relocates them in a narrative context. Their implications, however, remain the same. Indeed, the poem as a whole fictionalizes the main themes of "Mont Blanc," primarily through the use of the ascent and descent archetypes first employed in "Queen Mab." The synthesis thus effected between "Queen Mab" and "Mont Blanc" provides the imagistic and conceptual basis, not only for "Prometheus Unbound," but also for "The Witch of Atlas," "Adonais," and "The Triumph of Life."

Equally as important as the cave imagery in "The Revolt of Islam" is the proliferation of references to the water imagery of "Mont Blanc." There the mountain's peak, hiding as it does the source of the Arve, symbolizes the noumenal Power in its transcendent aspect ("Mont Blanc yet gleams on high:— the power is there" [l. 127]). But that Power is also immanent in life itself, as shown by its descent "in likeness of the Arve":

> Awful scene,
> Where Power in likeness of the Arve comes down
> From the ice-gulfs that gird his secret throne.
> ["Mont Blanc" ll. 15–17]

If the Power underlying sense objects is unknowable, the source of human perception is equally remote:

> The everlasting universe of things
> Flows through the mind, and rolls its rapid waves,
> Now dark—now glittering—now reflecting gloom—
> Now lending splendour, where from secret springs
> The source of human thought its tribute brings
> Of waters.
>
> [ll. 1–6]

"Things" are the objects of perception, "human thought" perception itself, and "mind" the interdependence of the two which is life. But the "secret springs" of thought, like the source of the Arve, cannot be known. Both in metaphor and idea, this passage draws upon the address to the stream in "Alastor":

> "O stream!
> Whose source is inaccessibly profound,
> Whither do thy mysterious waters tend?
> Thou imagest my life. Thy darksome stillness,
> Thy dazzling waves, thy loud and hollow gulfs,
> Thy searchless fountain, and invisible course
> Have each their type in me."
>
> ["Alastor," ll. 502–8]

Such passages powerfully illuminate Cythna's own psychic explorations in "The Revolt of Islam":

> "My mind became the book through which I grew
> Wise in all human wisdom, and its cave,
> Which like a mine I rifled through and through
> To me the keeping of its secrets gave—"[6]

This is the kernel from which Asia's descent into the cave of Demogorgon was to flower. Unlike Asia, however, Cythna seems to have unearthed the secrets buried in the cave of the mind. In the terms of "Prometheus Unbound" or "Mont Blanc" these secrets would be knowledge of noumenal reality. What are the secrets here? Like the "thrilling secrets" which the poet of "Alastor" discovers ("Alastor, l. 128), they are not specified; Cythna breaks off with a dash and begins a description of mind itself:

"One mind, the type of all, the moveless wave
Whose calm reflects all moving things that are,
Necessity, and love, and life, the grave,
And sympathy, fountains of hope and fear;
Justice, and truth, and time, and the world's natural sphere."
[7.31.3104-8]

If "Mont Blanc" makes the mind the channel for the flowing "universe of things," this passage makes it the reflector of that universe, a universe which includes not merely sense objects but also the entire range of conceptions (ll. 3106-8). In thus reflecting phenomenal reality each mind is the type of all that is; as well, perhaps as of all other minds. This is part of the secret knowledge Cythna has gained.

However, the secrets she discovers involve more than this, for they enable her to write in a new language, a language "subtler" than the one I now employ:

"And on the sand would I make signs to range
These woofs, as they were woven, of my thought;
Clear, elemental shapes, whose smallest change
A subtler language within language wrought."
[7.32.3109-12]

Ordinary language names the impressions and conceptions born of the mind's meeting with phenomenal reality. It also constructs and defines relations among these things. Cythna's, however, is an elemental "language within language," defining not only the relation between mind and phenomena, but also the nature of thought itself. The "key" of the "truths" Pythagoras possessed (l. 3114), it involves definition by symbols subtler than words; subtler than numbers or music, as well, because Pythagoras communicated his wisdom only "dimly" (l. 3113). These "clear, elemental shapes" are Shelley's ideal medium and, in obscurely describing it, he defines again the impossibility of portraying the source of our perception.

My reading of this passage clearly echoes Shelley's prose speculation on the impossibility of discovering the nature of our own thought, or at least of communicating that discovery:

If it were possible that a person should give a faithful history of his being from the earliest epochs of his recollection, a picture would be presented such as the world has never contemplated before. *A mirror would be held up to all men in which they might behold their own recollections and, in dim perspective, their shadowy hopes and fears.* . . . But thought can [only] with difficulty visit the intricate and winding chambers which it inhabits. It is like a river whose rapid and perpetual stream flows outwards. . . . *The caverns of the mind are obscure and shadowy;* or pervaded with a lustre, beautifully bright indeed, but shining not beyond their portals. If it were possible to be where we have been, vitally and indeed—if at the moment of our presence there, we could define the results of our experience—if the passage from sensation to reflection . . . . were not so dizzying and tumultuous, this attempt [to define the source of perception] would be less difficult.[7] (My italics)

Cythna visits the chambers of her own thought and defines the results of her experience.

The episode in canto 7 reveals, for the first time, the full import of Cythna's earlier allusions to submerged sources of hope and illumination. It is a moment of revelation for Cythna, if not for us, and it represents the consummation of her imaginative development. The narrative has, besides its overt sensational incidents, an inner drama of the mind which is developed with considerable skill. Shelley whispers his meaning in the abstruse language of Cythna's reflections, but can also shout it out clearly and unmistakably in her public orations, especially in stanzas 5 and 6 of canto 8, where Cythna, translating the "subtler language" of canto 7 into a coarser tongue, reveals the source of our thought to be inscrutable. This is what Shelley himself reveals in "The Revolt of Islam" as a whole, attempting to make metaphysical skepticism publicly attractive. The sensational incidents and melodramatic tone probably represent Shelley's estimation of public taste more than his own artistic preferences. As he says in his preface, he wrote the poem "in the view of kindling within . . . [his] readers a virtuous enthusiasm for liberty." It is, significantly, when "on holiday" that Shelley produces the masterpiece least flawed by shrill rhetoric: "The Witch of Atlas."[8]

But, whatever its deficiencies, "The Revolt of Islam" reveals Shelley using the ascent and descent archetypes with, for him, unprecendented subtlety and also continues the masterly portrayal of thought-object interdependence which "Mont Blanc" had initiated. Two distinct image-strands unify "The Revolt of Islam," the one portraying the inscrutability of first cause, and the other portraying the transcendence of time and space. In T. S. Eliot's terms, these represent "the way down" and "the way up" respectively. Both patterns converge in the twelfth-canto voyage of Laon and Cythna.

At the conclusion of "The Revolt of Islam," Laon and Cythna, with Cythna's child, voyage through a labyrinthine water world reminiscent of the landscape of "Kubla Khan." The voyage begins when the martyred couple awaken from death to find themselves beside a pool (ll. 4605–06) which springs from a submerged fountain (l. 4614). The fountain is submerged, not only beneath the water's surface, but also beneath flowers which spread their fragrance in the wind (ll. 4606–8) and, at a higher level, blossoms and fruit which appear simultaneously in this apocalyptic realm. These impressions produce intermingled light and shade on the pool's surface (l. 4611). Sloping to the submerged fountain are vast caves (ll. 4612–13) whose echoes, together with the fountain's spreading flood, produce a sounding discourse (ll. 4615–16). Waves are "bred" from the "strife" of waters in submerged caverns (ll. 4617–18) and channeled by a chasm to feed a deep river (ll. 4619–20). The submerged fountain is thus presented as the unseen hub of a universe of interrelated impressions, even as, in "Mont Blanc," the Arve's unseen source in the mountain's inaccessible peak accounts, both directly and indirectly, for all the impressions in the poem.

The presentation of this Mont Blancian landscape in canto 12 of "The Revolt of Islam" recapitulates the earlier portrayals of the relationship between an ineffable first cause and the universe of thought and its objects. It draws in, as it were, the descent thread of the preceding narrative, even as the portrayal of the voyage's conclusion redefines the earlier visions of ascent, transfiguration, and transcendence.

The voyage ends at a mountain-bordered lake (12.41.4811) from which Laon discerns the Temple of the Spirit, the Heaven which stands above this watery Eden. This temple is "like a sphere" (l. 4813) and emits a sound to which the boat responds, as if to the pull of gravity.[9] The sphere's sound directs the boat's motion in the same way that, for a Pythagorean anyway, music directs the courses of the stars.[10] Finally the "charmed boat" ascends to find "haven" in the temple's sphere (ll. 4814–76).

This presentation of the temple as the object of erotic ascent has been adumbrated already in the starlike appearance of Laon and Cythna. Like Prometheus and Asia after them, Laon and Cythna undergo transfiguration and possess a capacity for transcendence apparently denied the other characters. Their union, in any case, leads to their transcendence of the material world, and their martyrdom in canto 12 is partly an excuse for leaving that world behind.[11]

Of the two lovers, Cythna is the more frequently transfigured, in visual revelations of her divine nature. Before his removal from the world, Laon's perception of these transfigurations is often agonizing, since it lures him to the limits of mortal life. In this he resembles the Voice in the Air who addresses the transfigured Asia (2.5) as well of course as the disciples in the presence of the transfigured Christ. Cythna, as the object of erotic ascent, is portrayed in blinding light veiled by enigmatic imagery, imagery which suggests the confusion of the mortal mind in the presence of divinity:

> We lived a day as we were wont to live,
> But Nature had a robe of glory on,
> And the bright air o'er every shape did weave
> Intenser hues, so that *the herbless stone,*
> *The leafless bough among the leaves alone,*
> *Had being larger than its own could be,*
> And Cythna's pure and radiant self was shown,
> In this strange vision, so divine to me,
> That, if I loved before, now love was agony.
>
> [3.3.1126–34, my italics]

As so often happens in Shelley's writing, the ideas and metaphors in this rather obscure passage are clarified in a later poem. "The leafless bough" has "being larger than its own could be" because, like the Sensitive Plant, it possesses nothing and can therefore lose itself in the larger "being" which surrounds it. In a figure drawn from Socrates' description of Eros in *The Symposium*, "it loves, even like Love . . . / It desires what it has not, the Beautiful!" ("The Sensitive Plant" [1820], ll. 76–77).[12] Living only in its desire, the Sensitive Plant is a type of the human soul. Similarly, the leafless bough and the herbless stone are both Platonic "types" of Laon, who experiences "agony" here because his identity is lost in love for Cythna. Her "pure and radiant self" is, for Laon, the equivalent of the eternal Form of Beauty to which the soul aspires.

The passage describes the last moments Laon and Cythna share before, but newly past their childhood, they are separated. To summarize what follows: Cythna is captured and borne away by sea to become part of the tyrant Othman's harem (3), imprisoned beneath the Symplegades where she bears a child (7), rescued by mariners in whom she instills libertarian ideas (8), and borne back to the tyrant's city, which is ultimately destroyed by war (6, 10). During these spectacular episodes Laon is chained and starved in a deserted edifice (3), rescued by a Spenserian (or Coleridgean) hermit who bears him to his oversea cell (4), and, finally, in Othman's city, reunited with Cythna (5, 6).[13] The following passage picks up the story at this point: Othman's city is suffering plague and famine as a result of the war, and the priests are crying for vengeance on the freethinking reformers, Laon and Cythna, whom they blame for all their woes and whom they will ultimately martyr. In this passage, Laon gives Cythna a last look before offering himself up for the priests' vengeance:

> Her lips were parted, and the measured breath
> Was now heard there;—her dark and intricate eyes
> Orb within orb, deeper than sleep or death,
> Absorbed the glories of the burning skies,
> Which, mingling with her heart's deep ecstasies,
> Burst from her looks and gestures;—and a light
> Of liquid tenderness, like love, did rise
> From her whole frame, an atmosphere which quite

Arrayed her in its beams, tremulous and soft and bright.

[11.5.4261-69]

Both passages portray moments of imaginative perception. In the first passage Cythna's form is so "radiant" as to make Laon's love an "agony." His love is the erotic drive to transcendence and is agony because it can destroy the mortal man. The passage attempts to portray the interrelation of air with air (ll. 1128-30). This interrelation weaves "intenser hues" *over* "every shape" (ll. 1128-29). What one has here, then, is a woven veil of air visibly ("bright air") covering the objects of perception. But this veil does not dim perception—rather it heightens it (l. 1131, cf. "The Triumph of Life," ll. 29-33), thus revealing Cythna's essential divinity. Of course the entire process is enigmatic and confusing. How can air be visible? And, if visible, how can a veil of air clarify rather than obscure perception? The questions are unanswerable because the transcendent perception Laon attempts to describe is indescribable. This poetic admission of bewilderment is characteristic of Shelley's apolcalyptic skepticism, but this is the first poem in which it takes its later, familiar form (see the "Life of Life" lyric) of deliberate obscurity, a controversial tactic more successful here than in the Wagnerian stage directions of the second quoted stanza.

In this second passage, Cythna's eyes absorb the light of the sky. Cythna infuses this light with her inner happiness and expresses the resultant vision in emanating brightness which, unlike the light of the heavens, is suffused with the love of her inner response. Paraphrase is inevitably clumsy. It is clear in any case that Cythna transforms the environmental light into an image of "the white radiance of Eternity." Similar phenomena occur regularly throughout the poem, notably in 1.45.526-31; 4.30-31, 34; 5.24, 44, 52; 11.4-8. These passages all maintain the implication that Cythna is an earthly star. Throughout the poem Laon and Cythna are imaged as morning and evening star, two manifestations of one planetary light, even as their own divinity and that of the transcendent Temple of the Spirit are two manifestations of a divine Unity.

Venusian imagery is presented in great detail in the first canto and recurs fragmentarily in the subsequent portrayals of Laon and Cythna as stars (e.g., 9.35–36.3780–92). In the following passage from canto 1, Shelley has been transported by Cythna to the Temple of the Spirit. From this timeless perspective Laon relates the events which have led to his transcendent union with Cythna. The strategy is clearly reminiscent of "Queen Mab," Laon's narrative composing the main body of the poem. Before he can speak, however, Laon must be metamorphosed from the Luciferian snake which, with the morning star, is one of his earthly "types." In this metamorphosis Cythna, too, takes on her divine form:

> Then first, two glittering lights were seen to glide
> In circles on the amethystine floor,
> Small serpent eyes trailing from side to side
> Like meteors on a river's grassy shore,
> They round each other rolled, dilating more
> And more—then rose, commingling into one,
> One clear and mighty planet hanging o'er
> A cloud of deepest shadow, which was thrown
> Athwart the glowing steps and the crystalline throne.
> [1.56.622–30]

In stanzas 26 and 27 of this first canto Cythna reveals that the serpent she bears with her is Lucifer, the fallen morning star, while, in stanza 21, Cythna herself is closely associated with Vesper, the evening star. The quoted passage portrays Laon's metamorphosis from Luciferian serpent to star. In this resumption of their divine shape, the two meteors of Laon's serpent eyes intermingle to produce one planet which is neither Lucifer nor Vesper, but Venus; that is, the eternally abiding Form of that planet and that Love which is only fragmentarily perceived in the realm of time. I realize my language is Platonic, but there is still a substantial difference between versified Platonism and this transformation of Platonic ideas into an unique and individual myth.

The sustained perception of such a Form is beyond human capacity. This is why Shelley says that the Form is "fairer than . . . thought may frame" (l. 633) and why Shelley's halting description of the Form in lines 638 to 639 ends with a reference to his own faintness (l. 640). When Shelley revives he no longer perceives the one Form, but rather a male and a female figure—Laon and Cythna—the elements of the one Form, reduced, as it were, to comprehensible shape. Even now, however, in describing the female figure, Shelley can portray only the light which is filtered through her locks and her "gathered cloak" (l. 663). Even though weakened by the veil of cloak and hair, these lines of light are still "glances of soul-dissolving glory" (l. 664), and none except Laon can bear the direct light of Cythna's eyes (ll. 665–66). All these elements—the insistence on the inadequacy of language, the fainting, the veil—are familiar to readers of Shelley; too familiar, no doubt, to some. They are handled with less artistic success here than in "Prometheus Unbound," but one cannot adequately judge them without understanding that they dramatize the vision's ineffability; that their purpose is to portray the theme of skepticism, and not merely to "play up" an effect. The fragmented allusions to morning and evening star in the remainder of the poem recall this transcendent perception. When, addressing the crowd in canto 5, Cythna veils her own blinding light, it is to protect her mortal beholders from annihilation (5.46.2125–33). Even so, Laon, in his mortal form, swoons from his perception of the transfigured Cythna (l. 2115). Later manifestations of the same pattern occur in Asia's transfiguration and in that charming passage where the Witch of Atlas weaves a protective veil to shield her beholders from the full force of her radiance (8).

The literal-minded might well ask why Laon and Cythna, with their capacity for transcendence, should ever become embroiled in earthly affairs. The answer is that, like the Shelley of the "Hymn to Intellectual Beauty," they are reformers with a strong sense of mission. Laon and Cythna both know the falsity of religious and political dogma and, as with Shelley himself in the "Hymn to Intellectual Beauty," this knowledge *binds* them to "love all human kind" (Hymn, l. 84). Their pursuit of spiritual insight outside the pale of church and society recalls the spiritual quest of the equally independent hero of "Alastor." Like him, they are led to realize the ineffability of first cause.

Laon's childhood is virtually identical with Cythna's. The latter, in her fragmentary prologue to Laon's narrative (1.25–47), reveals how her earliest youth, like that of the "Alastor" poet, was dominated by a desire for occult knowledge (1.35.438; cf. "Alastor," ll. 76–77, 128) and how, again like the "Alastor" poet, she grew up in a natural environment "far from men" (1.36.442) where, like the Shelley of the dedication (5), she studied "divinest lore." She discovered this lore in books she had inherited from a "dying poet," "a youth with hoary hair" strikingly similar to the prematurely aged poet of "Alastor" (1.37.453–59). Moreover, like the Shelley of the "Hymn to Intellectual Beauty," Cythna gained from the natural environment otherworldly intimations which made her weep and "[clasp] . . . [her] hands . . . in ecstasy" (1.36.449–50; Hymn, l. 60). The issue of these experiences was, as in the Hymn, a radical iconoclasm:

> "Thus the dark tale which history doth unfold
> I knew, but not, methinks, as others know,
> For they weep not; and Wisdom had unrolled
> The clouds which hide the gulf of mortal woe,—
> To few can she that warning vision show—
> For I loved all things with intense devotion;
> So that when Hope's deep source in fullest flow
> Like earthquake did uplift the stagnant ocean
> Of human thoughts—mine shook beneath the
>   wide emotion."

[1.38.460–68]

"Hope's deep source" is the skepticism which precipitated the French Revolution, while "the stagnant ocean / Of human thoughts" is the dogmatic stupor which, before the French Revolution, had frozen European society into tyrannical hierarchies (1.39.469–77). The ocean-mastering current of Hope speaks through Cythna, just as the ocean-mastering West Wind becomes, through Shelley's lips, "the trumpet of a prophecy" ("Ode To The West Wind," ll. 36–42, 69). Cythna sets out for (presumably) Paris, where she tries in vain to prevent imaginative defiance from freezing into vengeance and renewed tyranny (44). During Laon's narrative, her address to the mariners who serve Othman recalls this messianic activity. Her address makes publicly accessible Shelley's descriptions of the Power in the essay "On Life," in

"Mont Blanc," and in canto 7. Clearly Cythna has intuited the
Power and knows its inscrutability:

> "'Ye feel and think—has some immortal Power
> Such purposes? or in a human mood,
> Dream ye some Power . . . builds for man in solitude?

> "'What is that Power? Ye mock yourselves, and give
> A human heart to what ye cannot know:
> *As if the cause of life could think and live!*
> 'Twere as if man's own works should feel, and show
> The hopes, and fears, and thoughts from which they flow,
> And he be like to them!'"
>
> [8.4–5.3232–40, my italics]

"It is infinitely improbable that the cause of mind, that is, of
existence, is similar to mind." But man imaginatively shapes the
mindless Power into his own form and worships that illusory
image as a reality:

> "'What is that Power? Some moon-struck sophist stood
> Watching the light from his own soul upthrown
> Fill Heaven and darken Earth, and in such mood
> The Form he saw and worshipped was his own,
> *His likeness in the world's vast mirror shown;*
> And 'twere an innocent dream, but that a faith
> Nursed by fear's dew of poison, grows thereon,
> And that men say, that Power has chosen Death
> On all who scorn its laws, to wreak immortal wrath.'"
>
> [8.6.3244–52, my italics]

Drained of imaginative energy, the mind duplicates its own hell by
imposing its dogmas on others. Just as the idyllic childhood of
Laon and Cythna employs the conventions of pastoral love poetry
to portray imaginative communion with nature, so this passage
internalizes hell to portray intellectual oppression.

The water imagery of canto 1, stanza 38 is sustained and developed throughout the poem, where the interrelation of fountain,
well, stream, river, and sea portrays life (e.g., 2.23, 6.34), while the
mirroring *Doppelgänger* imagery of superstitious worship portrays
the deadening effects of dogma (2.8; 8.5–10; 10.22, 26–27). Beneath
it all are the ineffable secrets of the mind's cave. Although these
secrets are mysteriously articulated in Cythna's "subtler lan-

guage," for us they must remain the unknowable "Power" of her oration.

"The Revolt of Islam," then, presents the premises of "Mont Blanc" within a framework which may be loosely termed "Platonic." Above time is the eternal Temple of the Spirit. Below time is the eternal mysterious Power. When Laon and Cythna unite as divine beings, as in cantos 11, 12, and 1, they ascend out of time toward or to the transcendent heaven. When, on the other hand, they unite as imaginatively inspired reformers, as in cantos 2 and 6, they descend toward the inaccessible source of life. The deluded ones, like the sophist of canto 8, find their dogmatic certainty mirrored in the heavens (8.6; 10.27–28), while the wise find salvation in intuition of life's unfathomable mystery (4.13, 15; 5.51–52; 6.30, 41). Since damnation is above and salvation below, the serpent becomes the icon of good and the eagle the icon of evil, a characteristic Romantic reversal (1.26–33). For Laon and Cythna, though, the way down is also the way up: skepticism sets them on the path of the political reformer, and their ministry brings them transcendence through martyrdom. Thus the voyage of canto 12—from subterranean fountain through life's flowing rivers to the couple's timeless union in the Temple of the Spirit—symbolically recapitulates the action of the poem as a whole and sketches out the different levels of its universe.

This fountain-river-star image-sequence is introduced from time to time during the complex narrative, as if to remind us of the abiding framework within which the triumphs and tragedies occur. In canto 9, for instance, Laon and Cythna, anticipating martyrdom, consider the nature of life and death (see epigraph). Cythna says:

> "Alas, our thoughts flow on with stream, whose waters
> Return not to their fountain—Earth and Heaven,
> The Ocean and the Sun, the Clouds their daughters,
> Winter, and Spring, and Morn, and Noon, and Even,
> All that we are or know, is darkly driven
> Towards one gulf."
>
> [9.35.3775–80]

Just as "it is infinitely improbable that the cause of mind . . . is similar to mind" so, to put it in another way, the fountain of our thoughts is beyond thought: it is the ineffable Power underlying both thought and its objects. As Shelley said in a passage earlier quoted: "[Thought] is like a river whose rapid and perpetual stream flows outwards:—like one in dread who speeds through the recesses of some haunted pile, and dares not look behind."[14] Here again is the skepticism which distinguishes his consideration of first causes. For a deeper consideration of the same question, one may return to the crucial soliloquy of the "Alastor" poet:

> "O stream!
> Whose source is inaccessibly profound,
> Whither do thy mysterious waters tend?
> Thou imagest my life. Thy darksome stillness,
> Thy dazzling waves, thy loud and hollow gulfs,
> Thy searchless fountain, and invisible course
> Have each their type in me: and the wide sky,
> And measureless ocean may declare as soon
> What oozy cavern or what wandering cloud
> Contains thy waters, as the universe
> Tell where these living thoughts reside, when stretched
> Upon thy flowers my bloodless limbs shall waste
> I' the passing wind!"
>
> [Ll. 502–14]

Life is the tapestry woven from thought and its objects. Just as the death of the "Alastor" poet will render it equally impossible to determine where the thoughts of his mind and the waters his mind perceives will "reside," so death will immerse both what Laon and Cythna "are" (thought) and what they "know" (thought's objects) in a dark "gulf" of oblivion. This gulf is what Shelley himself anticipates when, in the last stanza of "Adonais," he feels himself "borne darkly, fearfully afar."

This, however, is but half the tale, as both the last three lines of "Adonais" and the rest of canto 9 reveal. Cythna concludes her meditation:

> "But time shall be forgiven,
> Though it change all but thee!"—She ceased—night's gloom
> Meanwhile had fallen on earth from the sky's sunless dome.
>
> Though she had ceased, her countenance uplifted
> To Heaven, still spake, with solemn glory bright;

> Her dark deep eyes, her lips, whose motions gifted
> The air they breathed with love, her locks undight.
> "Fair star of life and love," I cried, "My soul's delight,
> Why lookest thou on the crystalline skies?
> O, that my spirit were yon Heaven of night
> Which gazes on thee with its thousand eyes!"
> She turned to me and smiled—that smile was Paradise!
> [Ll. 3781–92]

As Cythna prophesies her transcendent union with Laon, she becomes, in effect, the first star of evening—an earthly Vesper. In the last line her smile is paradise to Laon because he is Lucifer to her Vesper, sharing her divinity. The star imagery thus clearly anticipates the transcendence which will finally lift the couple out of time. Another crucial occasion where this image-sequence occurs is in canto 7, stanzas 30 to 32.

The imagery, then, is thematically consistent, if one accepts the hypothetical portrayal of a Mont Blancian universe within a quasi-Platonic framework. I suspect that, philosophically, this is an absurdity. Shelley, however, is concerned here with presenting "a genuine picture of [his] own mind," and his mind, to the very end of his career, felt both the drive to transcend earthly trouble and the drive to smash dogma and promote reform.[15]The "philosophical" perspectives are metaphors portraying that imaginative awakening and love which, to Shelley, was "the sole law which should govern the moral world."[16]

An understanding of the image-patterns and of the skepticism they express shows that the poem transcends the simplistic Manichaeism which critics, S. F. Gingerich and Wasserman among them, have ascribed to it.[17] It also explains Cythna's assertion that man himself could eliminate evil if he would forswear dogma (8.16–17.3334–51). The portrayal in canto 9 of Necessity forever binding evil with evil and good with good (l. 3709) describes historical time, not the timeless realm of the Power from which arise neither good nor evil, but rather the imaginative intimations to which man responds in both a positive and a negative manner. Significantly, the "Spirit of evil" is described as "one Power of many shapes which none may know" (1.27.361–62). Man himself creates evil by shaping the unknowable Power into idols. The first murderer observed the duel of snake and eagle while his own thoughts were at war (1.26.358). In the lines "when to the flood / That fair Star fell, he turned and shed his brother's blood" (1.26.359–60), the order of the events suggests that the fall of Lucifer preceded the first murder, but against this ambiguous metaphorical passage one must weigh Cythna's literal assertion that even natural phenomena such as death, earthquake, and mutability could "nought avail" if man would banish "Tyranny" and dogmatic "Faith" (1.29.385–86). The external manifestation of evil is the reflection, not the cause, of man's fall. Good and evil are not presented here as autonomous forces beyond human control. This Blakean optimism, far from manifesting a Manichaean resignation, represents the high point of Shelley's hopes for mankind, hopes which, in "Prometheus Unbound," have already begun to decline. Man's positive response to metaphysical skepticism would, if universal, break the historical chain of revolution and reaction and usher in the millennium. But "we let 'I dare not' wait upon 'I would,'" as Shelley reminds us in his "Defence of Poetry."[18]

"The Revolt of Islam" has fared badly at the hands of critics who, in their preoccupation with Zoroastrian Manichaeism, have ignored its relation to Shelley's other poems and to Romantic poetry generally.[19] Most critics who, like Barnard, have attempted to explore the philosophical implications of the poem, have drawn those implications from isolated analyses of individual passages, rather than from an examination of the total image-pattern, the myth it creates, and the place of that myth in the corpus of Shelley's work.[20] Despite Gothic lapses, the richly diversified images of this poem evince a new mastery in Shelley's tracing of "minute and remote distinctions of feeling."[21] The ideas, credible in their context, are consistent among themselves, creating that unity in diversity which "Queen Mab" so woefully lacks. While hardly on the level of "Prometheus Unbound" and the major poems which follow it, "The Revolt of Islam" is nevertheless, in imagery, in symbol, in narrative, and in theme, the paradigm against which their ironic variations are to be measured. The refinement, revision, and redefinition of this poem in Shelley's mature masterpieces is the backbone of his artistic achievement.

3 DARK MIRRORS

"Prometheus Unbound"

WHETHER it be King Lear confronting his Fool, Hamlet the skull of Yorick, or Don Quixote the mocking mirrors, the hero's sudden recognition of his own absurd image has produced some of literature's most disturbing moments. Suddenly to see oneself outside oneself, in a *Doppelgänger* image which reveals all that one has refused to acknowledge, can be at once pathetic, tragic, and farcical. That situation occurs, not once, but repeatedly, in "Prometheus Unbound," and focuses the meaning of the drama as a whole. As in "The Revolt of Islam" the mirror or *Doppelgänger* motif in "Prometheus Unbound" portrays the mind's imprisonment by self-created dogmas. In both poems psychic liberation occurs through iconoclastic skepticism.

Among the most significant of these *Doppelgänger* relationships is that of Prometheus to the phantasm of Jupiter. Prometheus, "made wise" by three thousand years of suffering (l. 58), decides that his initial hatred of Jupiter was untenable and resolves to recall the curse he first pronounced on his oppressor. In examining this part of act 1 (ll. 1–305), one should note the contrast between the accounts which the Earth gives of the underworld in her fallen and regenerate states. In act 1 her world of the dead is peopled by mechanical doubles of the living, whereas in act 3 it is (by implication, at least) an Elysium which makes this earthly existence resemble her original account of the underworld by comparison (3.3.113–14). From the death-realm of act 1 Prometheus summons the phantasm or double of Jupiter to pronounce his curse, not wishing the curse to "pass again" from his own lips or the lips "of aught resembling [him]"; i.e. his own phantasm.

The phantasm of Jupiter, with its attributes of calmness and strength (ll. 238, 259), seems to mirror the dominant traits of the fallen Prometheus's own character (l. 262). Its apparent "cruelty" and "coldness" (ll. 238, 258) are not qualities one associates with the Prometheus of act 1, but, upon hearing the severity of Prometheus's original curse, one realizes that the young Prometheus repaid the cruelty of his tyrant with an equally cruel longing for revenge, thus becoming, in effect, the double of his oppressor.[1] To this extent, the pronouncement of the curse in lines 262 to 301 presents Prometheus not only with his own youthful words, but also with an image of himself in his unregenerate youth. Ironically, the phantasm of Jupiter confronts Prometheus with his own youthful image in a way his own phantasm could not, since the latter, as Earth reveals (l. 203), represents Prometheus as he now exists, not as he existed in his youth.

The issues of Prometheus's confrontation with what is, in effect, his own youthful self are a realization of the extent of his original vengeful folly and a formal recantation of his curse. Thus the interrelation of the Titan with his youthful double serves both to strengthen the former in his repudiation of vengeance and to reveal to the audience the extent of his spiritual development in the years preceding curtain rise.[2]

The term interrelation may seem inappropriate in this context, since the phantasm, after all, is merely the passive instrument of Prometheus's will, having no comprehension of the words it speaks. However, since the phantasm of Jupiter, in speaking the curse, becomes, in effect, the embodiment of Prometheus's hatred, the curse episode serves as a dramatic device, portraying the final conflict of the vengeful and forgiving elements in Prometheus's character. In the meeting of these two elements, the former, represented by the phantasm of Jupiter, is not merely subdued by the latter, but also strengthens the latter by revealing clearly the fanatical hatred the forgiving spirit of Prometheus would unleash if it ceased to maintain its vigilance over his soul. Prometheus has given earlier intimations of the battle between vengeance and forgiveness which has been raging inside him and is only now being resolved on the side of forgiveness. In line 4, for instance, he refers to himself as beholding the universe "with sleepless eyes," but five lines later employs the phrase "eyeless in hate" in a context which makes it uncertain whether he describes himself or the hateful Jupiter. Moreover, his confident assertion in lines 49 to 51 that, at a fated future hour, Jupiter will be overthrown, contrasts sharply with his references to personal "despair" (ll. 15, 24). His mention of his own "scorn" of Jupiter in line 15 and of "disdain" and "exultation" in lines 53 and 57 are rendered far too convincing by their context to be totally banished by the token renouncing of hate in the latter lines.

The curtain, then, rises upon the climax of an internal struggle which has raged for three thousand years (l. 12), and the curse episode of the first act portrays not only the hatred of the youthful Prometheus, but also the conflict of the warring elements in Prometheus's soul. The result of this conflict is a commitment to forgiveness that comes from perception of the consequences of vengeance rather than from token allegiance to a principle.

Framing the *Doppelgänger* interrelation of Prometheus and the phantasm of Jupiter are the *Doppelgänger* relationships of Jupiter and Prometheus to their environment—relationships which are themselves mirrors of each other and thus imply the identity of the youthful Titan with his oppressor. Jupiter "change[s] good to [his] own nature" (l. 381); he shapes the entire universe into an image of the "fear" (l. 285) which obsesses him in his insecurity. Having doomed himself to solipsism, never able to break out of the prison of self, Jupiter converts his "infinity" to a "robe of envenomed agony" (ll. 288–89)—Prometheus's curse having been also a prophecy. Accordingly, for Jupiter, the dome of heaven and the dome of the skull become identical—prisons for the "all-miscreative brain" (l. 448) which, seeing in the universe the mirror of its own "self-torturing solitude" (l. 295), will gradually succumb to madness and despair (ll. 55–56, 282–301).

Here again, though, as in the confrontation between Prometheus and the phantasm of Jupiter, one has an *inter*relation of elements. The universe itself is altered by Jupiter's perception of it, and thus reinforces his solipsism, becoming progressively more like him as his tyrannical control is consolidated. The free men who once presented Jupiter with the antithesis of his own mentality have become worshippers and haters, fettered by the same "self-contempt" which tortures their master (l. 8). Prometheus, too, in his fallen state, returns Jupiter's hatred, thus presenting his oppressor with a mirroring image of himself—indeed, a true image of himself, since the shackles which bind Prometheus are forged not from metal but from hate and are the true form of the "burning gold" (l. 291) of Jupiter's kingship. The curse which Prometheus pronounced upon Jupiter was terrifying because it consummated Jupiter's dominion, eliminating all alternatives to his "hate mentality." This total dominion, if permanent, would have destroyed Jupiter as surely as Demogorgon finally does. It would have destroyed Jupiter through causing his solipsistic insanity (ll. 288–91), but it would have destroyed Prometheus as well, since all would have shared in Jupiter's madness.

Jupiter's solipsism, of course, is a spiritual sickness, not a philosophical position. Epistemologically, Jupiter is not a monist but an uncompromising dualist, and his icy realm is the Shelleyan version of the fallen Urizen's frigid kingdom in night six of "The Four Zoas." Unable to vivify "impressions blunted by reiteration" through the imaginative marriage of thought and its objects, Jupiter can define his identity only through the mechanical mastery of an environment he will never know.[3] This isolation, with its attendant emphasis on mastery, is focused most effectively in Jupiter's act 3 recollection of his marriage to Thetis. Jupiter can define his relation to Thetis only in terms of mastery and control:

> Thou didst cry, "Insufferable might!
> God! Spare me! I sustain not the quick flames
> The penetrating presence; all my being,
> Like him whom the Numidian seps did thaw

Into a dew with poison, is dissolved,
Sinking through its foundations."[4]

Jupiter obviously regards the reference to Sabellus as a great compliment—a mark of the degree of his domination.[5] Against this predator-prey relationship one should set the interrelating imaginative perceptions of Laon and Cythna in cantos 2 and 6 of "The Revolt of Islam" or the "harmonies" of Prometheus and Asia, who, united, derive mutual joy from the exploration of each others' "unexhausted spirits" (3.3.36–39). Both these relationship are analogues for the imaginative union of mind and environment, even as Jupiter's domination of Thetis parallels his mechanical coercion of an environment he believes to be no part of him.

The destruction one sees when looking at Prometheus from Jupiter's perspective is bad enough. But one discerns even worse delusion when studying Prometheus's relation to his oppressor. For the ultimate irony of Jupiter's "will to power" is that he has no will of his own. Jupiter, like the phantasm of Jupiter, is no more than Prometheus's objectification of his own fallen nature. The boast of the youthful Prometheus—"O'er all things but thyself I gave thee power, / And my own will" (ll. 273–74)—was truer than he knew. Jupiter, like the "prototype of human misrule" in "Queen Mab" or the "shade" of the "moon-struck sophist" in "The Revolt of Islam," is the creation of his victim's mind. The fall of Prometheus occurred when he came to ascribe autonomous existence to the objects of his thought. This dualistic position precluded the imaginative modification of the environment into a home and froze it rather into an imprisoning "external reality." In effect, then, Prometheus is Jupiter, chaining himself to the rock and maintaining his own bondage.[6] Prometheus's belief that Jupiter is an autonomous entity is only symptomatic of the degree to which he has objectified his environment. Unable to perceive the true nature of his fallen condition, Prometheus externalizes and deifies the dualistic principle which is merely the false creation of his own mind. A heuristic postulate for dealing practically with the environment has been exalted into an absolute.

In seeking textual clues to the true nature of Prometheus's dilemma, one is best advised to turn to the portrayals of his fall or enchainment. The first account of the fall is given by the elements who answer the Titan's request that his curse be repeated. The elements do not actually repeat the curse, but rather describe its effects, which included a darkening of the day (ll. 109–12) and a retreat of the winds to their frozen caves (ll. 103–6). The subsequent dialogue between Prometheus and the frozen Earth reveals that, prior to the fall, the planet bore "o'ershadowing woods," but that its lawns and streams are now covered by "frore vapours" (l. 121). Earth's account of Prometheus's birth suggests that Jupiter had dominion *before* the Titan's arrival (ll. 152–62). However, the binding of Prometheus aroused the Earth to hatred and began a period of unprecedented desolation (ll. 165–86) in which the barren elements, shrivelled by their own hatred, preserve Prometheus's curse as "a treasured spell" (l. 184)—the antithesis of those "spells" prescribed by Demogorgon as the keys to salvation (4.568–78).

In beholding the universe of the first act, one sees the very desolation Earth describes; so there can be no doubt about the accuracy of her description. However, there is an anomaly in her speech. She makes it quite plain that grief and hatred were the causes of the present desolation (ll. 177–79), yet she says that the elements of her planet guard Prometheus's hate-filled curse as a treasure (ll. 181–86). The desolating effects of the curse, described by the elements in lines 91 to 107, make this statement especially perplexing. Moreover, Prometheus's recollection of wandering through "o'ershadowing woods" drinking "life from [Asia's] loved eyes" (ll. 122–23) makes clear that there must have been a period between the time of his birth and the time of his enchainment when Earth bore rich foliage rather than the "thin leaves," "stones," and "frozen air" which she herself recalls (ll. 153–55). Furthermore, Earth's suggestion that Jupiter reigned *before* Prometheus's birth (ll.159–62) is flatly contradicted by the fallen Prometheus's own assertion that *he* gave Jupiter his power (l. 273), an assertion verified by Asia in act 2 (2.4.43–46). All that emerges conclusively from Earth's speech, then, is that the present desolation results, partly at least, from her hatred of Jupiter. This hatred is sustained by her recollection of the Titan's curse (ll. 152–86). Prometheus himself, then, has not only shrivelled the environment with his hatred, but has taught the elements of the universe a similar hatred which they now cherish, despite its desolating effects (ll. 181–84). Thus the planet itself has become an image of the unregenerate Prometheus, even as it is an image of the hate-filled Jupiter.

The unregenerate nature of the planet is brought into sharp focus by Prometheus's recantation of his curse. On hearing this recantation, Earth laments that her son is "fallen and vanquishèd" (ll. 311–13). Clearly the fallen Prometheus has made the environment a mirror of his own hate and is responsible for the fall of his own world.

Turning momentarily from the confused account of the fall in act 1 to Asia's description of the fall in act 2, one learns that the reign of Jupiter was preceded by that of Saturn. Saturn's reign saw the origin of time (2.4.34–35). The denizens of Saturn's kingdom (including Jupiter) lacked, among other things, "the thought / Which pierces this dim universe like light" (2.4.40–41). But Prometheus gave Jupiter "wisdom" (l. 44) and "the dominion of wide Heaven" (l. 46). Jupiter, though, abused this power, allowing hardships to descend upon his subjects (ll. 49–58). Seeing this, Prometheus taught man many protective arts, among them medicine (ll. 59–63), love (ll. 63–65), the use of fire (ll. 66–68), mining (ll. 68–71), speech (l. 72), philosophy (ll. 72–73), natural science (ll. 74–75), music (ll. 75–79), sculpture (ll. 80–84), astronomy (ll. 74–75), sea-transport and navigation (ll. 92–94), architecture and "urban planning" (ll. 94–97). As a reward for Prometheus's efforts, however, Jupiter bound him "in destined pain" (l. 100).

At this point in her narrative, Asia addresses herself to the problem of evil. She makes clear that, although Jupiter allows death, disease, and misfortune to plague mankind, he is not himself the source of these afflictions (ll. 100–109). Who, then, she asks Demogorgon, is ultimately responsible for the evil man suffers? The subsequent exchange contains the key to the drama's meaning:

> *Demogorgon:*
>   If the abysm
> Could vomit forth its secrets . . . But a voice

Is wanting, the deep truth is imageless;
For what would it avail to bid thee gaze
On the revolving world? What to bid speak
Fate, Time, Occasion, Chance, and Change? To these
All things are subject but eternal Love.

Asia:
So much I asked before, and my heart gave
The response thou hast given; and of such truths
Each to itself must be the oracle.

[2.4.114–23]

In seeking the source of evil, "each to [himself] must be the oracle."
In mastering "Fate, Time, Occasion, Chance, and Change," love
alone is efficacious. Asia has already learned as much from ques-
tioning her own "heart." Clearly, then, the source of evil is internal
and, in controlling time and mutability, the tools whereby evil
effects its ends, one must draw upon the strength of one's own
spirit. Here one recalls canto 7 of "The Revolt of Islam" (31–32)
where Cythna's "mind" becomes a "cave" giving her "the keeping
of its secrets," possessed of which she converts "Necessity" and
"the grave" from external forces into "woofs" of an imaginative
language, transforming the environment into an image of her
imaginative intimations, unfreezing the objects of her thought and
reshaping them into an expression of her transcendent insight. In
"Prometheus Unbound," once the process or imaginative reshaping has begun, Jupiter, as an object of thought, will quickly be
dissipated by the mind and the universe will cease to be a frigid
prison. "When shall the destined hour arrive?" Asia asks (l. 128).
But the imaginative insight she will bring Prometheus is already
drawing the hour near. Demogorgon prepares to dethrone the
tyrant (ll. 150–54).

Jupiter, then, has no power apart from Prometheus's mental
inertia. When one considers the identical effects of Jupiter and the
fallen Prometheus on their environment and the striking similarity
of the unregenerate Prometheus to both Jupiter and the phantasm
of Jupiter, the identity of Jupiter as an objectification of Prometheus's own fallen nature becomes more than probable. Still more
evidence of this identity appears as the drama proceeds.

Although Jupiter is Prometheus's own creation, Prometheus's relation to Jupiter nevertheless involves *inter*action, since the Titan's belief in the reality of his oppressor is necessary if his development from hatred to forgiveness is to have validity. Thus Jupiter, though a specter, nevertheless makes possible the birth of wisdom in his victim. Looking back over three thousand years of self-torture, Prometheus says: "I hate no more, / As then ere misery made me wise" (1.57–58). This moral victory is no less real for being the result of self-delusion. When Prometheus, imaginatively reawakened through union with Asia, steps down from the ghostly rock of his phantasmal universe, he takes with him a wisdom which could be achieved only within the delusory framework he leaves behind. Significantly, Demogorgon, when listing the "spells" whereby man may regain "empire" over the "doom" of a fallen world, has nothing to say of the imaginative awakening which ultimately liberates Prometheus, but speaks rather of forgiveness, love, and endurance (4.568–78).

Delusion, then, may morally strengthen its victim. In "Prometheus Unbound" Shelley's obsession with metaphysics produces an explanation of the problem of evil which, if unsatisfactory, is nevertheless as adequate a solution as one is likely to find to a problem ultimately insoluble. The idea that delusion and dogma may have value as crucibles of the soul partially explains the curiously tentative quality of mankind's regeneration in act 3. Unlike Laon, Prometheus is somewhat reluctant to leave this battleground of the spirit behind, and looks forward to witnessing mankind's future vicissitudes with an almost approving resignation (3.3.23–25). One can find no parallel to this attitude in either Laon or Cythna. In its attitude to evil the drama is less hopeful than "The Revolt of Islam," acts 3 and 4 suggesting that the pendulum of history may well swing forever between revolution and reaction.

The opening episodes of act 1 present *Doppelgänger* confrontations between Prometheus and the phantasm of Jupiter, between Prometheus and Jupiter himself, and between both Prometheus and Jupiter and their environment. Another significant instance of interrelation among mutually mirroring images in act 1 occurs when Prometheus is tortured by the Furies. The visions which the Furies present to Prometheus involve three instances of *Doppelgänger* confrontation. In these relationships the mutually mirroring images are the revolutionary Christ, mankind, and Prometheus himself.

The first mirror relationship, between the revolutionary Christ and mankind, illustrates Prometheus's principle that "evil minds / Change good to their own nature" (ll. 380–81). Prometheus makes this assertion in answer to Mercury's proposal that he placate Jupiter (ll. 353–79). The import of the cryptic remark is that Prometheus's refusal to requite Jupiter's hate is in itself a "keen reproach" (l. 393), since the tyrant will thereby perceive his failure to corrupt Prometheus's character. Prometheus's visions of Christ and of the French Revolution, however, reveal that not only "evil minds," but also fallen minds, morally indifferent though not necessarily evil, "change good to their own nature. " The implications of this realization prove agonizing for the Titan.

Lines 546 to 563 show that Christ's revolutionary defiance of idolatry led only to further idolatry after his death. Here, as in the "Essay on Christianity," the followers of Christ—harmless enough before the Master's arrival—are shown to have converted their departed Master's words to "swift poison" (l. 548) by making them a dogma and by persecuting all those who did not subscribe to their literal truth (ll. 546–55). Similarly, the iconoclastic devotion to "Truth" and "Freedom" which precipitated the French Revolution was superseded by dogmatic tyranny when the victorious revolutionaries, overcome by hatred of their oppressors, employed their newly won power to effect murderous vengeance (ll. 566–77). Thus "those who endure / Deep wrongs for man . . . but heap / Thousandfold torment on themselves and him" (ll. 594–96). Thus, too, when the overthrow of one tyranny is effected, "terror survives the ravin it has gorged" (ll. 618–19). Schooled in centuries of terror and persecution, fallen man adopts these methods as if by reflex when tasting victory over his oppressors. Thus "the good" who spearhead revolution are succeeded only by new tyrants when the revolution has been effected. Accordingly "the good" always "want power" while "the powerful goodness want"

(l. 626), and "all best things are thus confused to ill" (l. 628).

In this process of interrelation, the good man (Christ, for instance) rouses his fellows to defy dogma, only to be taught the bitter lesson that, in the final analysis, his followers merely substitute one dogma for another (ll. 554–55). In actuality Christ and his followers do not become *Doppelgänger* images in this process, but the *Doppelgänger* motif is present nevertheless, since the socially triumphant Christians paint the humble Christ in the image of the inflated prelate, while, from the perspective of Christ, the oppressed come to mirror the dogmatists they oppose.

These, however, are merely the outer mirrors of the glass prison. Looking upon the crucified Christ and witnessing man's perversion both of Christ's ministry and of the lofty ideals of revolution, Prometheus sees, as in a glass, his own situation. The universe for which he suffers has already revealed its continuing allegiance to Jupiter's religion of hate (ll. 306–13); Prometheus's relation to his universe thus parallels that of Christ to his unregenerate followers. Conversely, the agony of Christ in lines 597 to 612 results from his recognition of his own situation mirrored in that of Prometheus. Prometheus provides, for the crucified Christ, evidence that the perversion of iconoclastic defiance which followed His own ministry will be repeated till the end of time. Prometheus is thus the most potent cause of Christ's agony, and he begs Christ to turn His eyes away (ll. 597–99) because they implicate him for repeating the Savior's folly. This interrelation between Prometheus and Christ is the most powerful ruse the Furies could devise for securing the former's capitulation.

The third and most ironic process of interrelation portrayed here is that between Prometheus and mankind. Even as the French revolutionaries answered oppression with oppression, hate with hate, so Prometheus, for three thousand years, has been requiting the hatred of his oppressor. Prometheus's hatred, though at last renounced, is still harbored by the withered environment as "a treasured spell." Realization of the parallel between his own fallen nature and that of fallen man is no doubt a salient factor in "tearing up the heart / Of the good Titan" (ll. 579–80) as the vision of bloody France fades from his view. Moreover, since the fallen men of

Prometheus's vision are denizens of his own universe, it is evident that his own fall has played a part in maintaining theirs. Thus, again, the vision involves a process of interaction.

The chorus of spirits who speak after the Furies depart reveal a subtler element in this last interrelationship, an element which escapes Prometheus. The fourth of the six spirits in this chorus is the first character in the drama to define the true nature of Prometheus's unfallen state. The relevant passage merits quotation:

> On a poet's lips I slept
> Dreaming like a love-adept
> In the sound his breathing kept;
> Nor seeks nor finds he mortal blisses,
> But feeds on the aëreal kisses
> Of shapes that haunt thought's wildernesses.
> He will watch from dawn to gloom
> The lake-reflected sun illume
> The yellow bees in the ivy-bloom
> Nor heed nor see, what things they be;
> But from these create he can
> Forms more real than living man
> Nurslings of immortality!
>
> [ll. 737-49]

The poet of this passage is obviously not concerned with the objects of his thought per se, but only with their utility as elements for imaginative vision. The phrase "thought's wildernesses" evokes an image of the mind as a shadowy labyrinth. Here one thinks of Shelley's assertions in the "Speculations on Metaphysics": "The caverns of the mind are obscure, and shadowy . . . [Perception] is like a river [which] flows outward." One thinks too of "Mont Blanc," where the "tribute" of "human thought" comes from "secret springs"—the secret and inscrutable source of human perception which is the Power underlying life's interdependence of thought and thing ("Mont Blanc," ll. 4, 84–97). Equally relevant here is the image of Cythna "rifling" her mind like a "cave" (7.31.3101–4).

Such attempts to trace perception to its source issue in realization that the secret of life is inscrutable and that no one image can serve as an embodiment of the life-source (see "Mont Blanc," ll.

84–144). Equally important, however, is the attendant realization that "the power is there" ("Mont Blanc," l. 127) and that, inscrutable as it is, our realization of its existence alone gives meaning to the "earth and stars and sea" of "life's unquiet dream" ("Mont Blanc," ll. 127–44; "Hymn to Intellectual Beauty," ll. 25–36). Without our realization of the Power's existence the "dream" itself would be the only reality we could know.

Realization of the existence of the Power makes man reshape the objects of thought into hypothetical images of the life-source. Hence, for Cythna, "all moving things that are" become the "woofs" of an imaginative vision (7.31–32.3105–10). Hence, too, the poet of the above passage, after exploring "thought's wildernesses," creates from the "lake-reflected sun," "the yellow bees" (ll. 744–45), and the other objects of thought and perception, "forms" which, as images of the reality he intuits in exploring his own mind, are indeed "nurslings of immortality."

In the light of Shelley's preceding poems, this is the logical implication of the paradox that, although the poet has no interest in the objects of his thought for themselves (l. 746), he nevertheless creates from them "nurslings of immortality" (l. 749). This condensed and rather cryptic description of the imaginative process heralds in minor key the fuller portrayal of imaginative awakening in acts 2 and 3, even as the spirits' brief allusions to Spring (ll. 790–800) are taken up in the next act as dominant motifs.

The quoted passage is followed by another which constitutes the denouement of act 1, the true account of Prometheus's fall:

> *Chorus of Spirits:*
> Hast thou beheld the form of Love?
>
> *Fifth Spirit:*
> As over wide dominions
> I sped, like some swift cloud that wings the wide air's
> wildernesses,
> That planet-crested shape swept by on lightning-braided
> pinions,
> Scattering the liquid joy of life from his ambrosial
> tresses:
> His footsteps paved the world with light; but as I passed
> 'twas fading,

And hollow Ruin yawned behind: great sages bound in
  madness,
And headless patriots, and pale youths who perished,
  unupbraiding,
Gleamed in the night. I wandered o'er, till thou, O
  King of sadness,
Turned by thy smile the worst I saw to recollected
  gladness.

[Ll. 763–71]

Here, like the Christ of the Furies who "smile[d] on the sanguine
earth" (l. 547), the form of Love "paved the world with light"
(l. 766). The close connection between the "form of Love" and
Christ is emphasized by the planetary light imagery which in lines
731 to 732 attends the Christ who visits the studious sage (cf. the
"planet-crested shape" of Love [l. 765]). This sage is undoubtedly
among those who are "bound in madness" (l. 768) by religious
tyrants. The positive visions of the first three spirits, who witness
revolutionary heroism (ll. 694–707), efficacious self-sacrifice
(ll. 708–22), and devotion to the true Christ (ll. 723–36), are negated
in the above passage, where revolutionary heroism becomes
reactionary persecution (1.768), efficacious self-sacrifice becomes
meaningless martyrdom (ll. 768–69), and a devotion to true Christianity is punished by (presumably) the established church (l. 768).

Thus far, then, one has merely a recapitulation of the stupidity
portrayed earlier by the Furies. The rest of the passage, however, is
a demonic parody of the fourth spirit's vision and reveals the true
meaning of Prometheus's fall:

Sixth Spirit:
Ah, sister! Desolation is a delicate thing:
It walks not on the earth, it floats not on the air,
But treads with lulling footstep, and fans with silent wing
The tender hopes which in their hearts the best and gentlest
  bear;
Who, soothed to false repose by the fanning plumes above
And the music-stirring motion of its soft and busy feet,
Dream visions of aëreal joy, and call the monster, Love,
And wake, and find the shadow Pain, as he whom now we
  greet.

[ll. 772–79]

This passage directly parodies the vision of the fourth spirit. The poet of that vision, like the Shelley of "Mont Blanc" or the Cythna of "The Revolt of Islam," images his intimations in hypothetical visions which are "nurslings of immortality." The dreamers of the above passage, like that "luminary of the world" the "Alastor" poet, are among "the best and gentlest" of mankind. The form of Love here becomes Desolation: it causes the dreamers to create "visions" of their "tender hopes." While, in dream, these visions are sources of joy, in the light of day the dreamers' remembrance of them is painful. Like the pain-giving "shade" the "Alastor" poet pursues ("Alastor," l. 206), these aerial visions become agents of "the shadow Pain" when sought in the light of the sun. Clearly the dreamers regard their visions, not as "nurslings of immortality," as metaphorical images, but rather as objective entities to be adored for themselves. It is hardly surprising, then, that they awaken to find only "Pain."

The parallel here with the dream episode of "Alastor," even to the use of "love" as the agent of the dream (cf. "Alastor," ll. 203–5), is deliberately emphatic. This negative portrayal of the visionary dream also recalls the echoes of "Mont Blanc," "The Revolt of Islam," and other positive portrayals of imaginative creation in the fourth spirit's vision. The visions of the fourth and sixth spirits, taken together, recapitulate the positive and negative accounts of the imaginative process in Shelley's earlier verse.

Obviously the dreamers of the sixth spirit's vision are the agents of the desolation (l. 772) portrayed in lines 763 to 771. In these lines the consequences of dogmatic delusion are traced far beyond the limits of the personal tragedy in "Alastor." The dogmatic freezing of the mind's creations into "external realities" which occurs both in "Alastor" and in lines 772 to 779 is here shown to be the source of religious and political tyranny.

However, the dreamers of lines 772 to 779 are prototypes of Prometheus. Approaching the Titan, the sixth spirit says that the dreamers "Wake, and find the shadow Pain, *as he whom now we greet*" (my italics). One may reasonably conclude, then, that Prometheus, like the dreamers of lines 772 to 779, has objectified the creations of his own dreaming mind and, as a result, has found "the shadow Pain." And for Prometheus, as for the dreamers, the implication of this self-delusion extends far beyond the limits of personal suffering. Prometheus's dogmatic delusion, like that of the dreamers, has social, religious, and political consequences: indeed, he has frozen his entire universe into a state of sterile hatred.

In beholding the dreamers and then beholding Prometheus, the sixth spirit sees mirroring images of self-deception. If the spirit's vision of the dreamers focuses the true nature of Prometheus's fall, its vision of Prometheus focuses the Titanic implications of the dreamers' delusion. Religious, social, and political idolatry may attain universal dominion through the dreams of the innocent, should the innocent idolize the creations of their own minds. This is why "Desolation is a delicate thing." Mankind itself may create Titanic desolation, not through the machinations of its outcasts and criminals, but rather through dogmatic dream-worship by its "best and gentlest" (l. 775). The interrelation of Prometheus and the dreamers in lines 772 to 779 must ultimately take place in the mind of the reader, with the Titanic agony of the one and the "delicacy" of the others revealing the paradoxical relation between evil's source and consequence.

Having reached these conclusions, one may leave act 1 for a moment and briefly consider the theme of evil in the drama as a whole. Milton Wilson's suggestion that Shelley distinguishes between the evil inflicted on man by man and the evil inflicted on man by decay and mutability seems to me only partially valid, since the very concepts of time and death are hypothetical imagings of man's relation to eternity.[7] For Shelley, man is the slave of time and space only insofar as he regards them as the dimensions of an objectified environment. When man awakens to realization of the interdependence of thought and its objects and of the inscrutability of their relation to the Power underlying existence, time and space become mere veils of the imageless and inscrutable life-source.

This suggestion is supported by the concluding lines of the third act, where the Spirit of the Hour describes a regenerate mankind:

The painted veil, by those who were, called life,
Which mimicked, as with colours idly spread,

> All men believed or hoped, is torn aside
> The loathsome mask has fallen, the man remains
> Sceptreless, free, uncircumscribed—but man:
> Equal, unclassed, tribeless and nationless;
> Exempt from awe, worship, degree; the king
> Over himself; just, gentle, wise—but man:
> Passionless? no—yet free from guilt or pain,
> Which were, for his will made, or suffered them;
> Nor yet exempt, though ruling them like slaves,
> From chance, and death, and mutability,
> The clogs of that which else might oversoar
> The loftiest star of unascended heaven,
> Pinnacled dim in the intense inane.[8]
>
> [3.4.190–204]

The interdependence of thought and its objects here becomes the interdependence of man and the ideas of chance, death, and mutability. While the latter are controlled by man, it is evident that they control or affect him in turn: he is not "exempt" from them. But he *is* exempt from the enslaving effects of dogma. Millennial man ceases to worship images, thereby becoming "sceptreless," "free," and "uncircumscribed." Millennial man is "free from guilt or pain" because he has come to realize that "his will made or suffered them." Guilt is, for Shelley, the instrument whereby priests control their congregations, while the threat of pain keeps the tyrant secure over his slaves. But when man realizes that neither church nor state are divine institutions, he will cease to acknowledge both the validity of guilt and pain as instruments of persuasion and the authority of those whom his own will has invested with power. Thus the evil which man inflicts upon man disappears in the Promethean millennium.

Similarly, "chance," "death," and "mutability" can no longer inflict evil on man, since he now rules them "like slaves." Chance, death, and mutability are among the objects of thought. Thought without an object is unthinkable, but an object without thought is impossible. Man succumbs to delusion when he assumes that the objects of thought can have an independent existence, separate from the mind. The process of imaginative awakening is essentially the mind's seizing upon the objects of thought and reaffirming its dominion over "impressions" which have been "blunted by reiteration." But, in imaginatively seizing upon its objects, the mind may reshape those objects into images of ultimate reality. Thus "earth," "stars," "sea," and Mont Blanc may become veils of the inscrutable life-source. Thus, too, time may become the image and promise of eternity and death's relation to life may become the image of life's relation to afterlife, as the regenerate Earth reveals in her assertion: "Death is the veil which those who live call life" (3.3.113). Mutability and death become evils only if man wills it so.

Prevalent opinion to the contrary, this probing of the roots of evil in "Prometheus Unbound" is by no means Shelley's mature reassessment of a problem which, two years earlier, he had glibly explained away through a facile Manichaeism. The source of evil in "Prometheus Unbound" is identical with that in "The Revolt of Islam," where the problem receives subtle and detailed consideration. Cythna describes the imaginative activity which, during her imprisonment, saved her from hatred and despair, the two arch enemies of Prometheus:

> "My mind became the book through which I grew
> Wise in all human wisdom, and its cave,
> Which like a mine I rifled through and through,
> To me the keeping of its secrets gave—
> One mind, the type of all, the moveless wave
> Whose calm reflects all moving things that are,
> Necessity, and love, and life, the grave,
> And sympathy, fountains of hope and fear;
> Justice, and truth, and time, and the world's natural sphere.

> "And on the sand would I make signs to range
> These woofs, as they were woven, of my thought;
> Clear, elemental shapes, whose smallest change
> A subtler language within language wrought:
> The key of truths which once were dimly taught
> In old Crotona . . . "
>
> [7.31–32.3100–14]

"Necessity" and "the grave," "chance," "death," and "mutability," are seen here as objects of thought which, when imaginatively seized upon, cease to be external forces and become rather the "woofs" of an imaginative language. This language images "the key of truths" once taught by Pythagoras—truths possibly defining time's relation to eternity. Thus here, as in the passage quoted from "Prometheus Unbound," mind eradicates the evils of death and change by imaginative assimilation and expression.

Cythna is prompted to her imaginative expression by intimation of the Power underlying life. The descent of Asia to the cave of Demogorgon is intended to represent a similar intimation of the Power in "Prometheus Unbound." This intimation is the cause of the social regeneration described at the conclusion of act 3. In "The Revolt of Islam," this process of intimation and expression leads ultimately to transcendence, at least for Laon and Cythna. The planetary image which portrays transcendent union in the opening canto is echoed in the references to stars and to planetary music which, in subsequent cantos, both adumbrate and recall the couple's union. The second of the quoted stanzas, for instance, concludes with a reference to Laon's eyes which "shone through [Cythna's] sleep" like stars, "harmonizing" with her song. The image clearly foreshadows the transcendent union of the couple, where the evening star (Cythna) and the morning star (Laon) are blended into the eternal Form of Venus. The passage from "Prometheus Unbound" describes a communal imaginative awakening similar to the individual awakening portrayed in the stanzas from "The Revolt of Islam." It concludes with a reference to "the loftiest star of unascended heaven, / Pinnacled dim in the intense inane," and Asia, like Cythna, is associated with the planet Venus throughout the play. This imagery carries the same implications in "Prometheus Unbound" as in "The Revolt of Islam," and the cavern-star image-sequence which defines the limits of the cosmos of the earlier poem is repeated in the movement from subterranean cave to mountaintop transfiguration in the second act of "Prometheus Unbound."

One further comment is necessary on the passage quoted from act 3. At the conclusion of this passage, "death" and "mutability" are imaged as "clogs" preventing man's attainment of the transcendence to which "the loftiest star of . . . heaven" beckons him. Thus, despite my earlier assertions, man, like the Urania of "Adonais," would seem to be "chained to time" ("Adonais," l. 234).

This condition, however, prevails only in life. Death is a "clog" preventing transcendence only when it is viewed from the perspective of the living. In actual fact, death, as the regenerate Earth reveals (3.3.133–14), is the gateway to a condition of being which makes our present state seem death by comparison. It is not mutability alone, but rather mutability and all the other objects of thought, which prevent transcendence, since life is the interdependence of thought and its objects. This interdependence must be eradicated if man is to transcend life and attain "the intense inane," "the white radiance of Eternity." In the passage quoted from act 3, "chance," "death," and "mutability" are not merely forces preventing man from living through an endless succession of moments, but also objects of thought in the union of thought and thing which is earthly life. Trees, flowers, houses, stones, chickens, and mataphysics are just as culpable in "keeping man down" as are death and mutability. What the passage from act 3 portrays is a process of mutually sustaining interrelation between thought and its objects. Man "rules" the objects of his thought "like slaves" because he is able to shape them into imaginative visions. But he is "not exempt" from the influence of his slaves; indeed, he needs his "slaves" if he is to continue his earthly existence, since life is itself the union of thought and thing. This beneficial dependence of the master upon his slaves is the antithesis of the fallen Prometheus's enslavement to the creations of his own mind.[9]

In the light of these observations, how is one to regard the Prometheus of the first act? In his "Defence of Poetry" Shelley commented: "The tragedies of the Athenian poets are as mirrors in which the spectator beholds himself, under a thin disguise of circumstance, stript of all but that ideal perfection and energy which every one feels to be the internal type of all that he loves, admires, and would become."[10] Whatever the validity of this Nietzschean description of the Greek tragedies, it clearly bears an ironic relation to the "modernized" Prometheus of Shelley's first act, who may well present the spectator with all he fears to acknowledge in himself and in his society. Self-bound to a shadow-rock, imprisoned in a spectral inferno of his own making, the fallen Prometheus, were he an individual man and not an emblem of the race, would be, at worst, a dangerous figure, and, at best, a pathetically ineffectual dreamer, like Matthew Arnold's Shelley or the "Alastor" poet. But the individual's objectification of the environment, though it bring spiritual death to the individual, need not harm the other members of society, provided they are still able to marry thought and its objects in imaginative perception. Prometheus, however, with his imperial power, freezes the environment into the icy autonomy he believes it to possess and thus makes his own spiritual sickness the source of universal desolation. He focuses the worst evils of modern rationalism.

4 THE LIMITS OF VISION

"Prometheus Unbound" and "The Witch of Atlas"

THE mind's tendency to idolize its creations is the element of human corruption which most interested Shelley. The first act of "Prometheus Unbound" may be regarded as Shelley's consummate expression of this idea—it is virtually a theme and variations exploring all facets of the destructive interrelation between the mind and its creations.

The second act of "Prometheus Unbound" portrays the positive effects of imaginative awakening and stands in relation to the first act as *Paradiso* to *Inferno*. In place of the fanaticism, idolatry, and hatred which inform almost every episode in act 1, we have, in act 2, Asia's descent to the cave of Demogorgon. There she receives the renovating assurance that "the deep truth is imageless" (2.4.116). "Alastor," "Mont Blanc," and the Hymn all show how love must accompany awareness of an inscrutable first cause. The "deep truth" is the source of life. Awareness of its inscrutability prompts a vision of universal love which unites "all articulate beings" (2.5.35–36). The failure of the Voice in the Air to specify the appearance of the transfigured Asia (2.5.70–71) is not, as the New Critics have suggested, a symptom of artistic incompetence, but rather an idealization of the metaphysical uncertainty which precludes dogma and fanaticism and unites honest men in humility before life's mystery.[1] The Voice in the Air speaks for "all articulate beings" and what it articulates is its own "failure" (l. 70) to comprehend the "life of life" (l. 48), the essence beyond existence. This failure, if universally acknowledged, could eliminate dogma and realize the love and fellowship which are momentarily glimpsed in the paradise of this scene.

The third and fourth acts are poised between the negative and the positive visions of the first and second acts. Prometheus, in act 1, is a gigantic emblem of fallen man. The universal desolation his passivity causes is the Titanic analogue of the invididual man's idolatry. Conversely, the imaginative communion of Asia and Prometheus in act 2 is, like the union of Laon and Cythna in cantos 1 and 12 of "The Revolt of Islam," a hypothetical portrayal of a transcendence which man cannot experience while he lives. Act 1 of "Prometheus Unbound" descends to the nadir of mental passivity while act 2 approaches that humanly unattainable apex of imaginative activity in which the mind's divine nucleus or prototype, fully awakened, merges with transcendent reality.

The concept of an indwelling divinity which is the ideal and eternal part of man is articulated many times in Shelley's work; it is, for instance, the ideal "prototype" of his frequently quoted fragment "On Love":[2]

> We dimly see within our intellectual nature a miniature as it were of our entire self, yet deprived of all that we condemn or despise, the ideal prototype of every thing excellent or lovely that we are capable of conceiving as belonging to the nature of man . . . a soul within our soul that describes a circle around its proper paradise which pain and sorrow and evil dare not overleap. To this we eagerly refer all sensations, thirsting that they should resemble or correspond with it.[3]

In subsequent discussions of this indwelling "nucleus" Shelley describes the imagination, not as intuiting noumenal reality, but as molding phenomenal imagery into a reflection and complement of this "nucleus" or soul:

> Let it not be imagined that because the Greeks were deprived of its legitimate object, they were incapable of sentimental

love; and that this passion is the mere child of chivalry and the literature of modern times. This object, or its archetype, forever exists in the mind, which selects among those who resemble it, that which most resembles it; and instinctively fills up the interstices of the imperfect image, in the same manner as the imagination moulds and completes the shapes in clouds, or in the fire, into the resemblances of whatever form, animal, building, &c., happens to be present to it.[4]

The "legitimate object" of love to which Shelley refers here is ultimately not woman, but the transcendent divinity to which the soul aspires. Shelley's metaphors for this divinity are often drawn from Plato:[5]

It is eternal, unproduced, indestructible; neither subject to increase nor decay; not, like other things, partly beautiful and partly deformed; not at one time beautiful and at another time not; not beautiful in relation to one thing and deformed in relation to another; not here beautiful and there deformed; not beautiful in the estimation of one person and deformed in that of another; nor can this supreme beauty be figured to the imagination like a beautiful face, or beautiful hands, or any portion of the body, nor like any discourse, nor any science. Nor does it subsist in any other that lives or is, either in earth, or in heaven, or in any other place; but it is eternally uniform and consistent and moneidic [sic] with itself. All other things are beautiful through a participation of it, with this condition, that although they are subject to production and decay, it never becomes more or less, or endures any change.[6]

Although the subject of Shelley's Platonism is unfashionable at the moment, the Platonic cast of much of his writing is undeniable. Indeed, the shrill insistence on the inadequacy of comparison which occurs in this passage is the prevalent tone of his major poems from "Prometheus Unbound" to "The Triumph of Life." This tone intensifies the skepticism of his poetry as a whole. If he is not always skeptical about the validity of his vision, he is certainly skeptical about the power of words to embody it. Frequently, especially in "The Triumph of Life," he is skeptical about the validity of the vision as well.

However, there is no doubt that the transfiguration of Prometheus images man's eternal soul or essence. In the moment of transfiguration, the soul escapes earthly illusion and communes with a complementary transcendent divinity. This divinity is both the indefinable essence of Diotima's parable and the transfigured Asia whom the Voice in the Air celebrates. At the moment of transfiguration

> His pale, wound-worn limbs
> Fell from Prometheus, and the azure night
> Grew radiant with the glory of that form
> Which lives unchanged within.[7]

These act 2 transfigurations of Asia and Prometheus must surely be counted among the most original visions in English Romanticism. There is certainly nothing to match them in the last two acts of the drama, excepting the scene with Ocean and Apollo, a high point in English poetry.

The third and fourth acts of "Prometheus Unbound" are a vision of the best that man can do without transcendence. They focus, neither on the hell of Titanic passivity nor on the heaven of transcendent union, but rather on a state intermediate between the two—the state of the individual mortal. The irony of these last two acts results mainly from the static quality of their vision. What they portray is to some degree a purgatory. While mortal man may attain both the upper and lower limits of this purgatory, he can never escape it while he lives: an eternity of corruption is precluded by the revolution-reaction cycle of history, while the transcendent union of the mind's divinity with the divinity of what I will call the Forms is unattainable in earthly life.[8] This discovery is already faintly implicit in the evanescence of the transfigurations of act 2. But the visions of the first two acts, however qualified or mitigated, ultimately serve as hypothetical and unattainable projections between which the human drama of the concluding acts is performed. This drama has no climax; there is no guarantee of a permanent millennium. Against the optimistic prophecies of Cythna in canto 9 (25–26, 35) of "The Revolt of Islam" or the vision of historical progress in canto 6 of "Queen Mab" (l. 34 ff.), "Prometheus Unbound" sets the Earth's observation that "Death is the veil which those who live call life." According to the last acts, man's historical striving is a dream, and man's true awakening will be, not to a social millennium, but to a total transcendence of earthly existence.

Previously I have shown that Shelley viewed the process of imaginative awakening from two perspectives. These perspectives may be somewhat crudely designated as the empirical and the Platonic. From an empirical perspective, the imagination gives realization that the source of both thought and its objects is inscrutable. This realization prompts a repudiation of idolatry. From a "Platonic" perspective, imaginative awakening involves the mind's realization both of its essential divinity and of the kinship that divinity bears to a transcendent reality which may be metaphorically termed the realm of the Forms.

But, when the divine prototype within the mind is brought to sustained consciousness, it perceives more than kinship with the transcendent reality; perception becomes identity, since the divinity in the mind and the divinity of the realm of the Forms are in fact one, their separation being only a spatial metaphor for man's fallen state. When they are identified, mortal life, with its unreal shadows of the divine Forms, gives way to the Forms themselves. Thus a total awakening of the mind's divinity annihilates the mortal man.[9]

But, from an earthly perspective, imaginative awakening involves only an intimation of the mind's divinity, and not transcendent union. This distinction between imaginative intimation and transcendent union is portrayed in the contrast between Shelley's veiled perception of the Form of Venus in canto 1 of "The Revolt of Islam" and the union of Laon and Cythna into that eternal Form. "The Revolt of Islam" portrays the process of imaginative awakening from both "Platonic" and "empirical" perspectives. The transcendence of Laon and Cythna frames the "empirical" intimations in cantos 2 and 6, where the couple oppose tyranny. In the framework of the poem as a whole this social activity seems to have a purgatorial significance. Not until Laon and Cythna have planted the seeds of a millennial revolution through martyrdom (9.35–36) do they achieve transcendence.

The last two acts of "Prometheus Unbound" bear an ironic

relation, not only to the first two acts, but also to "The Revolt of Islam," since the suggestion in the earlier work that imaginative vision will ultimately usher in the millennium (9.25–28) is negated by the implication in the later poem that history is a pendulum, forever swinging between tyranny and social upheaval. If the social reform to which Laon and Cythna devote themselves is, for them, a purgatorial passage to the stellar union of cantos 1 and 12, it is also, for mankind as a whole, part of a journey to the eternal Spring imaged in canto 9. Social striving has significance in relation to this eternal Spring, and not in relation to transcendence. The union of Laon and Cythna in cantos 1 and 12 is an emblematic portrayal of something outside of history.

At the conclusion of "The Revolt of Islam," the tension between transcendence and continuing social struggle is not disturbing, since man's social striving is a progress toward the millennium. In "Prometheus Unbound," however, the prophesied union of Prometheus and Asia is set against a ceaseless historical cycle of revolution and reaction. In this poem, realization that "the deep truth is imageless" may issue only in an evanescent dissipation of dogma, never in a permanent millennium. Thus Shelley's skeptical perspective on imagination loses the significance it possessed in "The Revolt of Islam." In the last part of "Prometheus Unbound," and in the major poems that follow it, this development causes a shift of thematic emphasis. Shelley's attention is no longer focused primarily on the contrast between imaginative skepticism and dogmatic idolatry, but rather on the contrast between actual transcendence and mere intimations of transcendent reality. This theme qualifies the affirmation of the drama's conclusion, but finds its consummate expression in the urbane and subtle stanzas of "The Witch of Atlas." Thus the concluding acts are best examined in conjunction with "The Witch of Atlas."

There is a close parallel between the aesthetic, dreamlike quality of the Witch's behavior and the pastoral languor of the united Asia and Prometheus. Both "The Witch of Atlas" and the last two acts of "Prometheus Unbound" repeatedly imply that we are witnessing only a dream.

This parallel is clear in the similarity between the cave of the

Witch and that of the unbound Prometheus. The cave of Prometheus and Asia is overgrown with light-filtering "odorous plants" (3.3.11), is "paved with veined emerald" (3.3.13), and contains a fountain. The "frozen tears" of stalactites descend from its roof (l. 15) "raining forth a doubtful light" (l. 17). Outside the cave the "ever-moving air" is heard "whispering . . . from tree to tree" (l. 19). Similarly, the Witch's cave is "odorous" (ll. 154, 169), filled with "ever-blooming Eden-trees" (l. 170), and pervaded by "sounds of air" (l. 155). Her cave also contains a "dark and azure well" (l. 241) which, when stirred, flings "to the cavern-roof inconstant spheres / And intertangled lines of light" (ll. 244–45). It is obviously a dwelling which would suit Asia and Prometheus well. Both caves portray a Saturnian, prelapsarian state of being. [10] Both are retreats, womb-worlds of pastoral tranquillity.

Prometheus and the Witch manifest an extraordinary interest in art. The Witch's dismissal of the nymphs in stanzas 23 and 24 results from her realization that she is immortal and can achieve total union only with another divinity. Stanza 25 reveals the grief this realization causes her in a universe where there is no divinity to complement her own. In stanza 26, however, the Witch immerses herself in scholarship (l. 250) and poetry (ll. 252–56), and she spends the remainder of the poem in a frenzy of artistic activity. This activity is compensation for the union she can never achieve:

> All day the wizard lady sate aloof
> Spelling out scrolls of dread antiquity,
> Under the cavern's fountain-lighted roof;
> Or broidering the pictured poesy
> Of some high tale upon her growing woof,
> Which the sweet splendour of her smiles could dye
> In hues outshining heaven—and ever she
> Added some grace to the wrought poesy.
>
> [26.249–56]

With this fabulous embroidery one should compare that of Prometheus, Asia, and Ione, who, in the cave of their union, will "entangle buds and flowers, and beams / Which twinkle on the fountain's brim" (3.3.30–31).

In addition, however, the Witch's aesthetic attitude to the vicissitudes of human life provides a striking parallel with that of
Prometheus. After her voyages with the Hermaphrodite were
concluded, the Witch rested in her lake-built Antarctic palace,
where she heard:

> all that had happened new
> Between the earth and moon, since they had brought
> The last intelligence—and now she grew
> Pale as that moon, lost in the watery night—
> And now she wept, and now she laughed outright.
>
> [54.476-80]

This is virtually identical to the life Prometheus anticipates after
reunion with Asia:

> We will sit and talk of time and change,
> As the world ebbs and flows, ourselves unchanged.
> What can hide man from mutability?
> And if ye sigh, then I will smile; and thou,
> Ione, shalt chant fragments of sea-music,
> Until I weep, when ye shall smile away
> The tears she brought, which yet were sweet to shed.
>
> [3.3.23-29]

The activity in both these passages seems to provide superficial
diversion. If the reported vicissitudes of mortal life cause Asia to
sigh, then Prometheus will smile, to comfort her presumably, or
perhaps out of amusement at her concern. Prometheus himself
will "weep" over old songs, and the comforted Asia will in turn
comfort her husband, who nevertheless enjoys his melancholy (l.
29). The equivalence of "sea-music" and mutability as causes for
tears implies an aesthete's attitude to human misfortune. The
Witch's alternation of tears and mirth seems equally superficial,
and since it forms part of a catalogue of diversions ("These were
tame pleasures," l. 481), one may assume her interest in sublunar
life to be primarily aesthetic. Indeed, although the Witch, perceiv-
ing the effects of dogma (62), accurately diagnoses the cause of
man's distress (ll. 543-44), Shelley nevertheless informs us that
"little did the sight disturb her soul" (l. 545). Her interest in human
misfortune is a diversion, like that of Prometheus in the quoted
passage. I will return to this idea at the end of the chapter.

Alone and immortal, the Witch might well seize upon aesthetic experience as compensation for her lonely state. The motivation of the united Asia and Prometheus, however, is more obscure. Indeed, many critics would take issue with the idea that the Prometheus of act 3 seems, in some respects, a detached aesthete.[11] However, there are further suggestions of this in his reunion speech:

> We will entangle buds and flowers, and beams
> Which twinkle on the fountain's brim, and make
> Strange combinations out of common things,
> Like human babes in their brief innocence;
> And we will search, with looks and words of love
> For hidden thoughts, each lovelier than the last,
> Our unexhausted spirits; and like lutes
> Touched by the skill of the enamoured wind,
> Weave harmonies divine, yet ever new,
> From difference sweet, where discord cannot be.
> And hither come, sped on the charmed winds,
> Which meet from all the points of heaven, as bees
> From every flower aëreal Enna feeds,
> At their known island-homes in Himera,
> The echoes of the human world, and tell
> Of the low voice of love, almost unheard,
> And dove-eyed pity's murmured pain, and music,
> Itself the echo of the heart, and all
> That tempers or improves man's life, now free;
> And lovely apparitions,—dim at first
> Then radiant, as the mind, arising bright
> From the embrace of beauty (whence the forms
> Of which these are the phantoms) casts on them
> The gathered rays which are reality—
> Shall visit us, the progeny immortal
> Of Painting, Sculpture and rapt Poesy,
> And arts, though unimagined, yet to be.
> The wandering voices and the shadows these
> Of all that man becomes, the mediators
> Of that best worship love, by him and us
> Given and returned; swift shapes and sounds, which grow
> More fair and soft as man grows wise and kind,
> And veil by veil evil and error fall.
>
> [3.3.30–62]

In lines 49 to 56, Prometheus describes how works of art are created by man. The "lovely apparitions" of line 49 are the objects of human perception, sublunar "phantoms" (l. 52) of the eternal "forms" (l. 51) composing the Platonic Heaven. The mind, "arising bright" (l. 50) from its intimation of the divine realm, re-creates its perceptions to reveal their true identity as shadows of the divine Forms; it thus "casts on them / The gathered rays which are reality" (ll. 52–53). Intimations of the Forms are as "the interpenetration of a diviner nature through our own" causing us to "dissolve, diffuse, and dissipate" our impressions "in order to recreate" them imaginatively.[12] The mind "casting forth" the "gathered rays" of its intimation is "as a fading coal," momentarily illumining its perceptions with divine light. The results are "Painting," "Sculpture," "Poesy," "and arts, though unimagined, yet to be" (ll. 55–56).

Lines 59 to 60 show that artistic creations will serve as "mediators" of a "love" "given and returned" between men and the united immortals. Art, then, will perform the mediating function exercised by Panthea in act 2. Just as Asia, focusing upon Panthea, was able to behold both her own reflected divinity and that of Prometheus (2.1.114–26), so man, focusing upon the objects of perception the "gathered rays" of his transcendent intimation, will see in the art he creates both his own reflected divinity and a shadow of the forms (see also 4.126–28, 412–17).[13] But the divine immortals, though giving and receiving love, will definitely not "dwell with" men.[14]

Why not? Why this emphasis on the mediating power of art instead of a portrayal of the united immortals dwelling among their people? Clearly Shelley retains his skeptical qualifications even in his portrayal of the millennium. Despite its pastoral tranquillity, the scene brings human limitations into sharp focus by placing them in the perspective of the immortals.

However, to maintain this perspective alone on the human drama of the last acts would be categorically reductive. The speech of Prometheus gives not only a sense of human limitation, but also a sense of man as happy *within* his limits. Just as the "lovely apparitions" of line 49 are "dim at first," so the "low voice of love" is at first "almost unheard" in the mortal world. Each subsequent episode of act 3 makes it louder; brings it closer to the fullness of well-being which informs the opening exchange of Ocean and Apollo. Each episode presents particularized natural description with a sense of sophisticated artifice; we are repeatedly drawn into the pastoral life only to be lurched out of it by an awareness of the urbanity with which it is described. We move constantly between the rustic perspective of liberated man, who is joyful both because he is free and because he is ignorant of his limits, and the sophistication of the gods, who see the mortal shepherds from the vantage point of their own immortality.

The Earth, for example, promises Asia and Prometheus a cave to dwell in. Around it there are orchards:

> Bright, golden globes
> Of fruit, suspended in their own green heaven;
> And, through their veined leaves and amber stems,
> The flowers whose purple and translucid bowls
> Stand ever mantling with aëreal dew.
>
> [3.3.139–43]

But near it is a pool:

> The windless and crystalline pool,
> Where ever lies, on unerasing waves,
> The image of a temple built above,
> Distinct with column, arch and architrave
> And palm-like capital, and overwrought,
> And populous with most living imagery—
> Praxitelean shapes, whose marble smiles
> Fill the hushed air with everlasting love.
> It is deserted now, but once it bore
> Thy name, Prometheus; there the emulous youths
> Bore to thine honour through the divine gloom
> The lamp, which was thine emblem . . . even as those
> Who bear the untransmitted torch of hope
> Into the grave across the night of life
> As thou hast borne it most triumphantly
> To this far goal of Time.[15]
>
> [3.3.159–74]

Both passages are from the 65-line speech which concludes the scene. The tone of the initial description is sensuous; the Earth relishes the fullness, the intense life of the vegetation ("ever mantling with aëreal dew"). What she perceives in the temple, however, are poise, removal, stillness ("windless," "crystalline," "image," "unerasing"). Twice the reference to imagery occurs, and both times it causes tension. The "image" or watery reflection "of a temple" (l. 161) is not the same thing as a temple, and to be "populous with most living imagery" (l. 164) is very different from being simply "populous." The temple, like Keats's Grecian urn, is "overwrought" with images and, like the little town on the urn, "it is deserted now" (l. 167). The last five lines compare three things: the runners bearing their torches in the lampadephoria; man bearing his torch of hope through the night of life into the grave; and Prometheus bearing his hope through ages of oppression to "this far goal of Time." The terms of the comparison show very clearly that the "far goal of Time" for man is transcendence and that transcendence is attained through the grave. The very term "goal of Time" suggests the millennium, but Earth says nothing of that here, because nothing man accomplishes in life bears comparison with the achievement of her son. Thus the tone of pastoral joy is ultimately tinged with the sense of limit; the sense that man must die to be finally free.

This is, at least, one implication of Earth's speech. Recalling her earlier description of the temple's origin, one sees why the temple must remain deserted:

> There is a cavern where my spirit
> Was panted forth in anguish whilst thy pain
> Made my heart mad, and those who did inhale it
> Became mad too, and built a temple there,
> And spoke, and were oracular, and lured
> The erring nations round to mutual war,
> And faithless faith, such as Jove kept with thee;
> Which breath now rises, as amongst tall weeds
> A violet's exhalation.
>
> [3.3.124–32]

As the product of Earth's hate, the temple was a place of dogmatic worship—the kind of worship Jupiter demanded. But the temple bore the name of Prometheus, not Jupiter, and, in light of this, the rites of "the emulous youths" (l. 168)—indeed, the very references to "name" (l. 168) and "emblem" (l. 170)—appear negative. "Faithless faith" (l. 130) is fanaticism, "faithless" because it breaks faith with the mind. What replaces it now is "that best worship love" (l. 59), a "faith" which is perhaps more literally "faithless" in the sense of not being dogmatically fixed. The conclusion of Earth's speech, with its vision of the distant temple, hints at the ease with which the second faith can revert to the first. For surely there is regret in the observation that the temple "is deserted now" (l. 167), and wistfulness in the tone of the description. This speech sets imaginative humanism against dogmatic worship and shows the mortal attraction of the latter. Thus the Dionysian references (e.g., ll. 148-57, cf, 2.3.1-10) are as double-edged here as the Olympian references in the "Ode to a Nightingale" or the "Ode to Psyche."

This subtle balancing of tone and implication is especially crucial in an act which forswears rhyme. "Prometheus Unbound" as a whole is filled with curses and incantations in rhyming stanzas. From the lines in which the phantasm of Jupiter repeats Prometheus's curse to those in which Demogorgon speaks the "spells" of social salvation, rhyme encloses effectual spells—what may be called *fiat-speech*. Of course much ineffectual speech is also placed in rhyming stanzas: the Furies' temptations of Prometheus, for example, or the lament of the Earth that her son "lies fallen and vanquished." But, whether effectual or ineffectual, most "spell-speech" in the drama occurs in stanzas. Act 3 is unique in the play, being entirely in blank verse. It is also the only act without fiat-speech. That is: no one in the act *says* anything which changes time or space; which transforms either the world or the course of events. Jupiter comes close to spell-casting in his defiance of Demogorgon, but this ineffectual sputter is a poor substitute for the satanic defiance of act 1. "What art thou?" he twice asks Demogorgon (3.1.51, 69), thinking that if he can name him he can curse or, if need be, worship. But the old order has passed away and, with it, both curses and worship. Ultimate reality refuses human shape (3.1.21-23, 51) or human categories (3.1.52, 69-70), even as the language of act 3 resists the closed finality of rhyme. When Prometheus himself transforms the Earth, he does so, not by speech, but by kissing her. Soon afterward the Spirit of the Hour releases the voice in Asia's nuptial shell. In both cases there is no spell; rather, we hear an account of effects: Earth describes her awakening; the Spirit of the Hour a changed society. Similarly, the Earth herself, recalling her oracular powers, describes the influence of her spells (3.3.124–32), but does not repeat them. Since the act consists almost entirely of reports, there is a danger of monotone. The act overcomes this danger by its tension between "urbane" and "rustic," immortal and mortal, perspectives.

Act 3 makes frequent use of a homely, familiar tone for which the other acts provide no parallel. This tone is most apparent in the naïve, eager speeches of the Spirit of the Earth. Note, for example, the spirit's longest speech in scene four (ll. 33–85), beginning with his claim that he is "grown wiser," although still remaining a child. For almost twenty lines we are given an awkward, explanatory preamble for the spirit's report of the millennium. The *well* which finally begins this report is casual and ingenuous ("Well, my path lay lately through a great city," l. 51), as is the "so they were" with which he excitedly answers his own rhetorical question (l. 75). The spirit is not at home in the city, and his metrically clumsy rhetorical question heightens his tone of rustic simplicity:

> and when the dawn
> Came, wouldst thou think that toads, and snakes, and efts,
> Could e'er be beautiful? yet so they were,
> *And that with little change of shape or hue.*
>
> [3.4.73–76, my italics]

What the spirit relishes is actual: no shape changes, no spectacle; rather, the natural environment. And the happier he is, the more detailed his perception grows:

> I cannot tell my joy, when o'er a lake
> Upon a drooping bough with nightshade twined,
> I saw two azure halcyons clinging downward
> And thinning one bright bunch of amber berries
> With quick, long beaks.
>
> [3.4.78–82]

The nightshade has lost its sting in the pastoral paradise.

Such close natural description specifies exactly the "change" which is the act's central concern. An equally difficult kind of pastoral simplicity occurs in Prometheus's echoes of King Lear:

> We will sit and talk of time and change,
> As the world ebbs and flows, ourselves unchanged.
> What can hide man from mutability?
>
> [3.3.23–25]

Prometheus's simple reunion speech, following upon his satanic defiance, is obviously meant to parallel Lear's purgatorial movement from outrage to hard-won calm. But, while Lear's pastoral speech sets his inner calm against his actual precarious position, Prometheus's speech links inner calm and actual security: as a god, he really *is* beyond mortal strife. The tone of near-sentimental resignation in this speech is repeated nowhere else in the play, although the speech's tranquillity is far surpassed in the flawless scene with Ocean and Apollo.

Prometheus's speech closes more strongly than it begins because it creates a dramatic tension between the divine and the human planes. The opposition of immortal and mortal perspectives is much less overt here than when Earth laments that her son is "fallen" or when the Voice in the Air "fails" in communing with Asia, but for that very reason the control of it may have required a surer hand. By restricting himself to blank verse—to one medium, as it were—Shelley shows his awareness of the "minute . . . distinctions of feeling" with which he deals.[16]

Repeated distinctions between image and reality focus the tension between the mortal and the divine. As earlier noted, Prometheus says that, in future, works of art will be "mediators" of a "love . . . given and returned" (3.3.59–60) between men and immortals. But these works, the "voices" and "shadows" of "all that man becomes" (ll. 57–58) will be mere "phantoms" (l. 52) of the "forms" of beauty (l. 51). As such they will represent a transitory, repeatedly renewed, communion—not a dogmatic and static ritual.

But it is worth repeating that the united immortals, though giving and receiving love, will not "dwell with" men. Man's imaginative communion is more than dogmatic worship, less than transcendent union. The immortals will remain apart and "unchanged" (l. 24) while "the world ebbs and flows" (l. 24), far away from them. As the act proceeds the facts of communion and separation are alternately emphasized.

On the positive side, Prometheus, free from his chains, can bend down to the Earth and awaken her with his love (l. 83 ff.). But Asia, by contrast, remains puzzled about "earthly" life: she cannot understand the word "death" as mortals understand it (ll. 110–14). In act 2 Demogorgon tailored his answers to Asia's understanding, and Asia questioned him as if she were a delegate of mankind. But now the distance between men and Titans receives as much emphasis as their imaginative communion.

Because of the gulf between immortal and mortal, the gods and spirits in act 3 are often like royalty in disguise. The liberated men, in turn, resemble naïve shepherds, while the Earth combines both royal and rustic qualities. Where once her speech shrivelled the environment and drove men mad, she now revivifies nature (ll. 131–32). Knowing both mortal and immortal speech (1.138–40), the Earth moves between an unambitious delight in man's condition and a wistful awareness of his limitations.

The act's thematic tension is especially clear in the spirits' development of themes introduced by Prometheus. The last part of the act repeatedly qualifies the word *change*, humanizing and intensifying a discussion "of time and change" (3.3.23) which began in godly detachment. "We shall not all sleep, but we shall all be changed," says Saint Paul. [17] What each man fears in the Last Judgment is the revelation of hidden evil; what he desires is a new spiritual body. But, after the sounding of Asia's shell, the new body turned out to be the old, and the "disguise" which vanished was the "evil nature" (3.4.77) engendered by tyranny:

> and those
> From whom [it] passed seemed mild and lovely forms
> After some foul disguise had fallen, and all
> Were somewhat changed, and after brief surprise
> And greetings of delighted wonder, all
> Went to their sleep again.
>
> [3.4.68–73]

There is only "brief surprise" because "the man remains" (l. 193), revealing his true, as opposed to his evil, nature. Man is not innately depraved. But, by the same token, he is not totally changed, either: he does not transcend his mortal limitations.

The Spirit of the Hour spends over one hundred lines exploring this distinction. Her entire concluding speech is an amplification of her statement that "there was a change" (l. 100). Although she has seen the love-fire of the second-act transfigurations "folded . . . round the sphered world" (l. 103), "given and returned" in mortal communion, she also envisions her "moonlike car" (l. 111) in its solar pantheon, surrounded by statues which "mock" all time and change. In the temple itself both transcendence and mediation are portrayed. The "moonlike car" and "amphisbaenic snake" have been agents of change in the past, although they are now imagined in the temple, before the smiling statues. The statues express love (l. 114). Like the art works of scene 3 or the atmospheric fire, they are "mediators," agents of communion. Among them are the sculptures of the spirit's steeds. The steeds themselves, however, are outside the temple, *in* the sun (l. 108) "where they henceforth will live exempt from toil" (l. 109), even as Prometheus promises Asia that "henceforth we will not part" (3.3.10).

The passage encapsulates the complex of relationships between eternity and time in the act as a whole. Since only imagination may mediate for man, his temple must be a museum of sculptures, not a pantheon of gods. Outside the temple, however, beyond the love-fire of the atmosphere, burns the flame of transcendence, the inaccessible sun. To this goal mortal runners, like the fiery steeds, bear their torch across the night of life.

After this divine vision the spirit "floated down" to earth (l. 106) and, not surprisingly, was at first "disappointed not to see / Such mighty change as [she] had felt within / Expressed in outward things" (ll. 128–30). A divinity in disguise among mortals, a queen among the shepherds, the spirit accommodates her royal expecta- tions to man's capacity, and finally considers man's condition, not in relation to eternity, but in relation to his previous enslavement (l. 130 ff.). In this light men appear free, and they *are* happy. But the phrase "expressed in outward things" (l. 130) is important. Men and women are happy because they have ceased to worship their creations. The "abandoned shrines" (l. 189) which cover the earth are now "but an astonishment" (l. 176): curiosities, perhaps only dimly understood.

Whether or not the true significance of the deserted temples is understood, a sense of limited vision intensifies the tension between the spirit's royal perspective and man's. It is surely anomalous, for example, that the instruments of coercion have not been removed or destroyed and, indeed, are generally "unregarded" by men (l. 179). If "unregarded" means "unconsidered," then this long description anticipates Demogorgon's later reminder that freedom must be vigilantly maintained. Man is without class, tribe, nation, or religion (ll. 195–96); he is "exempt" from these things, but, unlike the transcendent coursers, he is not "exempt from toil" because "chance and death and mutability" must be constantly ruled (ll. 201–2). These are the three objects of thought most likely to prompt a reinstitution of dogma, an end to imaginative freedom. Paradoxically, these are also the distinguishing features of mortal uncertainty, invalidating all dogmatic seals. In the third stanza of the "Hymn to Intellectual Beauty" Shelley says that religious categories are

> Frail spells—whose uttered charm might not avail to sever,
> From all we hear and all we see,
> Doubt, chance, and mutability.
>
> [Ll. 29–31]

The individual mind must not "oversoar" its limits (l. 202) with claims of absolute knowledge: sculptures, not idols; visions, not dogmas, are required.

But the shifting perspective of the spirit is what is most interesting here. She descends from a heavenly vision to the pastoral millennium, looks about, comments omnisciently, and then turns her vision back to "unascended heaven" (l. 203). And with this redirection of vision she epitomizes the very tendency which can destroy skeptical thought and imaginative freedom. For her eyes are not on the love-fire of the atmosphere but on the unchanging star beyond. Like Shelley at the conclusion of "Adonais," she turns her vision away from man to transcendence. As a spirit, she faces no danger in doing so. But her speech shows clearly that man himself *does* face danger in seeking "the intense inane." By closing the speech with her focus on the star, she leaves us in Eden with our eyes turned upward. When we awaken from the spell of her two-edged blank verse, we may well wonder if she has been admonisher or temptress.

Although I have already considered the conclusion of the act in the previous chapter, I wish to emphasize its repeated qualification. Man is "sceptreless, free, uncircumscribed—but [still, only, merely] man" (l. 194). Man is "just, gentle, wise—but [after all] man" (l. 197). The free men who are described are happy because they do not know their limitations. The onlookers, meanwhile, find them delightful, but limited. The immortals are like royalty or like interplanetary visitors at a rustic festival. Their praise is enthusiastic, but qualified by their superior knowledge.

The praise in act 4 is much shriller than that in act 3, as the planets and stars join the festival. Here the Spirit of the Earth is where he belongs: among the celebrants, rather than the spectators. As Panthea and Ione observe his sleep, their remarks close on an ironic note, but the dual perspective does not fully emerge until Demogorgon's concluding prophecy. Demogorgon warns that man may fall again (4.562–69). Demogorgon is the master of ceremonies, the play's first mover, neither god nor man. When he announces the possibility of renewed suffering and oppression it is not to be taken lightly: it is perhaps the most important statement in the play. Demogorgon foresees no permanent millennium, but let us more closely consider the one that exists. What makes it impermanent?

It is based on ignorance. The "tools / And emblems of its last *captivity*" (3.4.176–77, my italics) still stand on the earth, "unregarded now" (l. 179), but not destroyed either, ready to be used again. The "tomes / Of reasoned wrong" (ll. 166–67) which justified oppression are now "but an astonishment" (l. 176). But nothing has taken their place. Although science and technology flourish (4.135–74, 270–423), there is no final knowledge of anything; there are no metaphysics. If man grows tired of ignorance, if he formulates a final answer, a dogma, only once, the millennium will end. In the meantime it is man's ignorance of eternity which makes his rustic joy so charming to the immortal, and wistful, visitors. Prometheus never does occupy the royal temple, only the cave, but this does not mean that the temple has been opened to all men. On the contrary, it remains closed. Each man is left the temple of his own imagination, but that is a decidedly different thing. Shelley is not a poet of merely rhetorical gestures; more than most poets he means what he says and says precisely what he means. He will unite his hypothetical gods with one another, but not with man, and he leaves the temple closed because he knows what comes of creeds and temples. He portrays the millennium of a skeptic.

Prometheus's deserted temple, overwrought with "Praxitelean shapes," has its parallel in the lake-built palace where the Witch of Atlas takes her repose (48–54). The Austral lake which bears up the Witch's palace is a "haven," removed from the vicissitudes which plague mortal beings (ll. 441–47)—the symbol in fact of the Witch's immunity from the "weltering" of time's "restless tide" (l. 552). Similarly the temple of "Prometheus Unbound" is "built above" (3.3.161) a "windless and crystalline pool" (l. 160) and, in picturing it, the Earth imagines man bearing his torch of hope "into the grave across the night of life" (l. 172). Prometheus's deserted temple shows the inaccessibility of the "intense inane." It is deserted for the same reason that the Witch's dwelling is so remote: man would make it a place of sacrifice and idolatry. The once-oracular cave beside it, however, is a reminder of men's weakness, their need for temples. Perhaps the reason Demogorgon says that man may fall again is that the Earth's "oracular vapour" originally issued from his cave (2.3.4). We already know from act 1 how this vapor affects the world (1.177–86). There are no war cries now, only violets and thick grass (3.3.131–47), but Demogorgon reminds us that the Earth's face is always changing.

However, if, as the Earth says, life is no more than a dream preceding transcendent awakening, man's wars matter little. Man is too limited for them to matter. The Spirit of the Earth, emblem of man's new life in the Promethean millennium, rides dreaming on its planetary chariot:

Panthea:
And from the other opening in the wood
Rushes, with loud and whirlwind harmony,
A sphere, which is as many thousand spheres,
Solid as crystal, yet through all its mass
Flow, as through empty space, music and light:
Ten thousand orbs involving and involved,
Purple and azure, white, and green, and golden,
Sphere within sphere, and every space between
Peopled with unimaginable shapes,
Such as ghosts dream dwell in the lampless deep,
Yet each inter-transpicuous, and they whirl
Over each other with a thousand motions,
Upon a thousand sightless axles spinning,
And with the force of self-destroying swiftness,
Intensely, slowly, solemnly roll on,
Kindling with mingled sounds, and many tones,
Intelligible words and music wild.
With mighty whirl the multitudinous orb
Grinds the bright brook into an azure mist
Of elemental subtlety, like light;
And the wild odour of the forest flowers,
The music of the living grass and air,
The emerald light of leaf-entangled beams
Round its intense, yet self-conflicting speed,
Seem kneaded into one aëreal mass
Which drowns the sense. Within the orb itself,
Pillowed upon its alabaster arms,
Like to a child o'erwearied with sweet toil,
On its own folded wings, and wavy hair,
The Spirit of the Earth is laid asleep,
And you can see its little lips are moving,
Amid the changing light of their own smiles,
Like one who talks of what he loves in dream.
Ione:
'Tis only mocking the orb's harmony.[18]

[4.236–69]

The interrelation of the ten thousand orbs to form this Ezekiel-chariot (ll. 236–43) harmonizes many sounds into one tone (ll. 237, 240) and many hues into one kaleidoscopic light (ll. 240–43).[19] This combination of apparently lifeless elements encloses the "inter-transpicuous" and "unimaginable" shapes which, as reminders of Asia's "shapes too bright to see" (2.5.108),

perhaps suggest the spirits of a transcendent heaven. The shapes
are, in any case, alive, since their interrelation "kindle[s]" "intelligible words and music wild" (l. 252). As the vision moves from
the tenuous to the tangible one sees the "multitudinous orb"
incorporate a diverse array of natural impressions in "one aëreal
mass / Which drowns the sense" (ll. 260–61). The orb unites all the
objects of perception into one incomprehensible dance. Panthea
concludes her halting description of the chariot with a reference
to her failing sense perception (l. 261). Since she has already
identified the Spirit of the Earth as "the delicate spirit / That
guides the earth through heaven" (3.4.5–6), she knows the significance of what she witnesses:

> From afar
> The populous constellations call that light
> The loveliest of the planets; and sometimes
> It floats along the spray of the salt sea,
> Or makes its chariot of a foggy cloud,
> Or walks through fields or cities while men sleep,
> Or o'er the mountain tops, or down the rivers,
> Or through the green waste wilderness, as now,
> Wondering at all it sees. Before Jove reigned
> It loved our sister Asia . . .
> . . . .
> . . . . and with her
> It made its childish confidence, and told her
> All it had known or seen, for it saw much,
> Yet idly reasoned what it saw.
>
> [3.4.7–22]

A rustic in the pastoral festival, the spirit has always "idly reasoned
what it saw." The Olympian humor of Panthea's vision in act 4 lies
in the spectacle of the charioteer "that guides the earth through
heaven" being charioted, asleep, amidst a complexity it could
neither guide nor fathom.

The Spirit of the Earth sleeps amid the planet's measureless
impressions even as man sees the universe only through the narrow "chink" of his perception.[20] The spirit's childish dream mocks
the orb's difficult harmony and is mocked, in turn, by an order it
cannot grasp. Like the babe of William Blake's "Infant Sorrow" or

like Blake's Thel, the Spirit of the Earth is confined to an infantile existence in which the transcendent union of the immortals remains a fantasy impossible of fulfillment. Asia explains as much to the spirit in one of the drama's least successful passages:

> *Asia*:
> And never will we part, till thy chaste Sister
> Who guides the frozen and inconstant moon
> Will look on thy more warm and equal light
> Till her heart thaw like flakes of April snow
> And love thee.
> *Spirit of the Earth*:
> What, as Asia loves Prometheus?
> *Asia*:
> Peace, Wanton—thou art yet not old enough.
>
> [3.4.86–91]

This coy exchange is prophetic of the fourth act, where the male Earth sings a love duet with the Moon (hence the "moonlike car" of the *female* Spirit of the Hour [3.3.64–70, 3.4.111]). The spirit is enamored of the moon-goddess, after all, and a dream of "what he loves" (4.268) would surely include her. The description of the sleeping spirit is like Demogorgon's prophecy: it casts an aura of reverie over the closing festivities, as if they were not real. The Spirit of the Earth is the emblem of mortal man and his dream is the dream of life as described by the revivified Earth:

> The dewmists of my sunless sleep shall float
> Under the stars like balm; night-folded flowers
> Shall suck unwithering hues in their repose;
> And men and beasts in happy dreams shall gather
> Strength for the coming day and all its joy:
> And death shall be the last embrace of her
> Who takes the life she gave, even as a mother
> Folding her child, says, "Leave me not again!"
> *Asia*:
> Oh, Mother! wherefore speak the name of death?
> . . . .
> *Earth*:
> . . . .
> Death is the veil which those who live call life:
> They sleep, and it is lifted.
>
> [3.3.100–14]

In Prometheus's revivified universe, the Earth is a mother who nurses man through the dreams of his mortal sleep. Prometheus's liberation does not so much awaken the universe as it makes one aware of man's infantile slumber, at the same time making man himself more comfortable in his sleep by dispelling the nightmares of act 1.

There is a striking similarity between the Spirit of the Earth, as portrayed in lines 261 to 269 of act 4, and the Hermaphrodite who accompanies the voyaging Witch of Atlas:

> And ever as she went, the Image lay
> With folded wings and unawakened eyes;
> And o'er its gentle countenance did play
> The busy dreams, as thick as summer flies,
> Chasing the rapid smiles that would not stay,
> And drinking the warm tears, and the sweet sighs
> Inhaling, which, with busy murmur vain,
> They had aroused from that full heart and brain.
> [40.361–68]

The Hermaphrodite is the Witch's greatest artistic creation. It is a second spirit of the Earth, complete with "folded wings" (cf. 4.264), dreaming slumber (cf. 4.265), and infantile smiles (cf. 4.266–67). Both through her power to create such a being and through her similarity to the transfigured Asia, the Witch emerges as a poetic embodiment of the divine. Through its similarity to the Spirit of the Earth, the Hermaphrodite emerges here as an emblem of that limited consciousness which renders life a sleep. The impossibility of union or fellowship between the Witch and her creature is equivalent to the spirit's unfulfilled yearning for the divine.

All this further underscores the skepticism: Shelley qualifies not only his characters' statements but also the pastoral conventions both poems employ. For an important part of the pastoral convention, especially the pastoral interludes in Shakespearean drama, is vicarious wish fulfillment.[21] Unrequited love is an important part of the convention, too, and the union of ideal lovers is itself a wish-fulfillment dream. But Shelley emphasizes the element of reverie so strongly that the reader is repeatedly forced to consider the limitations of both art and dreaming.

The Witch's revivification of the corpse, for example, is not Gothic or morbid; like everything she does, it is aesthetically pleasing. Yet her creation exists midway between art and life, and parodies both:

> And there the body lay; age after age,
> Mute, breathing, beating, warm, and undecaying,
> Like one asleep in a green hermitage,
> With gentle smiles about its eyelids playing,
> And living in its dreams beyond the rage
> Of death or life; while they were still arraying
> In liveries ever new, the rapid, blind
> And fleeting generations of mankind.
>
> [71.609–16]

Here both art and eternal life are parodied.[22] Just as the Witch can "take her way" "beneath the . . . restless tide" of mortality (ll. 550–52), or as even Asia and Prometheus, in their divine languor, can "sit and talk of time and change, / As the world ebbs and flows, [themselves] unchanged," so the corpse "live[s] in its dreams beyond the rage / Of death or life" (ll. 613–14). In all three cases the advantages of immortality might be questioned. The "generations of mankind," "rapid, blind / And fleeting" though they be, consummate their mortal love and go to the grave in peace. But the Witch, eternally creating and eternally alone, is herself as permanent, and as static, as her creations. And are Prometheus and Asia to spend eternity in that cave with their sighs and sea music? If so, they are little more than gigantic reflections of the dreamers they observe. Of course one can choose to be ironic about *any* vision of eternity: one can ironically ask if the angels in Saint John's vision of Heaven are to spend eternity singing hymns. But it is not the same thing. Saint John does not deliberately undercut his assertions, nor follow his Apocalypse with a series of increasingly ironic variations of its vision. The tension latent in act 3 of "Prometheus Unbound" becomes virtually explicit in "The Witch of Atlas," where the uneasy meeting of fire and water, eternity and time, is the major theme.[23] Prometheus and Asia, like all artistic creations, *are* gigantic reflections of man. Shelley's dissatisfaction with the limits of art prompts not only deliberate obscurity and poetic admissions of inadequacy, but also the ironic mirrorings, parodies, and qualifications whereby he forces us to scrutinize his characters with the same mixture of empathy and detachment Keats used in recreating the urn. In this, his technique is consistent with his thought: his efforts to detach us grow logically out of his skepticism.

According to the "Defence of Poetry" inspiration is like "the interpenetration of a diviner nature through our own," a momentary illumination in the dream of life, bringing the divinity in the mind to light. The divine Witch can momentarily awaken the divinity in the minds of sleeping men:

> She, all those human figures breathing there,
> Beheld as living spirits—to her eyes
> The naked beauty of the soul lay bare,
> And often through a rude and worn disguise
> She saw the inner form most bright and fair—
> And then, she had a charm of strange device,
> Which murmured on mute lips with tender tone,
> Could make that Spirit mingle with her own.
>
> [66.569–76]

The stanza ironically refocuses the dream vision of the "Alastor" poet or of the sixth spirit who visits Prometheus (l.772–79). Stanza 68 shows the evanescence of the Witch's visitation. There we learn that "Among those mortal forms the wizard-maiden / Passed with an eye serene and heart unladen" (68.591–92). The "interpenetration of a diviner nature" is a moment in eternity for us, but from the perspective of eternity it is insignificant. The Witch's nonchalance in stanzas 66 and 68 has its Promethean equivalent in the detachment with which the united immortals learn of mortal vicissitudes (3.3.23–25) or contemplate communion with mankind (3.3.40–62).

To turn for a moment to a more positive perspective: a comparison of the following passages from "The Witch of Atlas" and "Prometheus Unbound" reveals a marked similarity between the effects of Prometheus's liberation and of the Witch's temporary intervention in human affairs. The first passage continues the account of the Witch's activity among sleeping mortals:

And she would write strange dreams upon the brain
Of those who were less beautiful, and make
All harsh and crooked purposes more vain
Than in the desert is the serpent's wake
Which the sand covers—all his evil gain
The miser in such dreams would rise and shake
Into a beggar's lap—the lying scribe
Would his own lies betray without a bribe.

The priests would write an explanation full,
Translating hieroglyphics into Greek,
How the god Apis really was a bull
And nothing more; and bid the herald stick
The same against the temple doors, and pull
The old cant down; they licensed all the speak
Whate'er they thought of hawks, and cats, and geese,
By pastoral letters to each diocese.

The king would dress an ape up in his crown
And robes, and seat him on his glorious seat,
And on the right hand of the sunlike throne
Would place a gaudy mock-bird to repeat
The chatterings of the monkey.—Every one
Of the prone courtiers crawled to kiss the feet
Of their great Emperor, when the morning came,
And kissed—alas, how many kiss the same!

The soldiers dreamed that they were blacksmiths, and
Walked out of quarters in somnambulism;
Round the red anvils you might see them stand
Like Cyclopses in Vulcan's sooty abysm,
Beating their swords to ploughshares—in a band
The gaolers sent those of the liberal schism
Free through the streets of Memphis, much, I wis,
To the annoyance of king Amasis.

And timid lovers who had been so coy
They hardly knew whether they loved or not,
Would rise out of their rest, and take sweet joy
To the fulfillment of their inmost thought;
And when next day the maiden and the boy
Met one another, both, like sinners caught,
Blushed at the thing which each believed was done
Only in fancy—till the tenth moon shone;

> And then the Witch would let them take no ill:
> Of many thousand schemes which lovers find
> The Witch found one,—and so they took their fill
> Of happiness in marriage warm and kind.
> Friends who by practice of some envious skill,
> Were torn apart—a wide wound, mind from mind!—
> She did unite again with visions clear
> Of deep affection and of truth sincere.
>
> [72–77.617–64]

These brilliant stanzas give us both wish fulfillment and icono-clasm with a vengeance. Here the Witch is like one of Oberon's company, enchanting and transforming the fallen court. All these incidents have their Promethean parallels. With the somnambulis-tic conversion of the soldiers into men of peace one may compare the nocturnal metamorphosis witnessed by the Spirit of the Earth:

> I hid myself
> Within a fountain in the public square,
> Where I lay like the reflex of the moon
> Seen in a wave under green leaves; and soon
> Those ugly human shapes and visages
> Of which I spoke as having wrought me pain,
> Passed floating through the air, and fading still
> Into the winds that scattered them; and those
> From whom they fled seemed mild and lovely forms
> After some foul disguise had fallen, and all
> Were somewhat changed, and after brief surprise
> And greetings of delighted wonder, all
> Went to their sleep again.
>
> [3.4.61–73]

The "ugly human shapes" include the "self-loved ignorance" (3.4.43) of the tyrant and his followers. Both in this passage and in the blacksmith episode of "The Witch of Atlas," this selfishness is expelled by the awakened "prototype"—the "mild and lovely [form]" of line 69 and the "naked beauty of the soul" revived by the Witch in stanza 66. In both poems the awakening results from the interpenetration of a diviner nature into the souls of the sleepers. The sleepers respond with a momentary repudiation of dogmatic authority, as well as of greed ("Witch," 72), idolatry (73–74), cus-tom (76), and envious self-love (77).

These effects are portrayed somewhat more solemnly in "Prometheus Unbound" than in "The Witch of Atlas." The repudiation of kingship and idolatry is described both by the Spirit of the Hour (3.4.164–89) and by the various singers of the "Ode to Joy" in act 4 (ll. 93–128, 338–55, 382–405). The Earth, in *his* list of defeated evils, includes not only kingship and idolatry but also the self-love the Witch's influence dispels:

> Leave Man, who was a many-sided mirror
> Which could distort to many a shape of error
> This true fair world of things, a sea reflecting Love;
> Which over all his kind, as the sun's heaven
> Gliding o'er ocean, smooth, serene and even,
> Darting from starry depths radiance and life, doth move.
> [4.382–87]

This mirror reference is a restatement, in major key, of the drama's central unifying motif. Man's mind is a refractive mirror when it remolds the objects of thought into a hypothetical image of that divine love intuited in imaginative awakening. When man worships this refracted image as the object of desire he distorts the "world of things" into a "shape of error," into an idol like the god Apis or a tyrant like the king whom the soldier-blacksmiths once served. This destructive interrelation of thought, its objects, and its imageless source was what caused Prometheus's fall.

Similarly, the envy and haughtiness which separate the "friends" of "The Witch of Atlas" are imaged as "satellites" of the human will. When worshipped as "guide" the will leads man astray, but when put to the service of love the will guides man to happiness. Man then becomes:

> One harmonious soul of many a soul,
> Whose nature is its own divine control,
> Where all things flow to all, as rivers to the sea;
> Familiar acts are beautiful through love;
> Labour, and pain, and grief, in life's green grove
> Sport like tame beasts, none knew how gentle they could be!
>
> His will, with all mean passions, bad delights,
> And selfish cares, its trembling satellites,
> A spirit ill to guide, but mighty to obey,

Is as a tempest-wingèd ship, whose helm
Love rules, through waves which dare not overwhelm,
Forcing life's wildest shores to own its sovereign sway.
[4.400–11]

Both here and at the beginning of "The Witch of Atlas" (5, 6) life is a "green grove" where love tames the wild beast. When brought to light, the love buried in the mind gains mastery over the will. Then the "blindly-working will" ("Queen Mab," 9.5) fulfills man's dreams; it becomes Ariel and Earth the enchanted island. The result, as portrayed in lines 412 to 423, is scientific and artistic mastery—the Promethean equivalent of the beating of the swords of the envious will into the ploughshares of love and peace ("The Witch of Atlas," l. 645). The harmony of love and will in the individual prompts a communal imaginative awakening. Man becomes "one harmonious soul of many a soul" and, as such, is able to subdue the universe (4.135–74, 406–23).

Besides the "selfish cares" which separate friends, love also subdues the "mean passions" of line 406. Among these "mean passions" are the lust and greed for which man enslaves woman and through which woman enslaves man ("Queen Mab," 5.189–93). The church's answer to this dilemma is the restrictive custom which in lines 653 to 656 of "The Witch of Atlas" causes the lovers guilt and shame. The *Witch's* answer to this dilemma, however, is an awakening of the divine love buried in the minds of the separated sleepers. Through this love "mean passions" are dispelled. Men and women meet as equals, rather than in the predator-prey relationship of Thetis and Jupiter. This theme finds expression not only in the passages quoted but also in the banishment of "pride," "jealousy," "envy," and "ill shame" described by the Spirit of the Hour (3.4.153–61). The beating of swords into ploughshares in "The Witch of Atlas" also has its Promethean parallel in the reillumination (see 2.4.64–99) of geological and other scientific discoveries by the rock-cleaving beams of the Spirit of the Earth (4.270–318).[24]

However, the parallels between "Prometheus Unbound" and "The Witch of Atlas" are ultimately ironic. The second poem develops and emphasizes the ironies in the first and the social regeneration in both poems is impermanent. The dance of the spirits in act 4 is ecstatic, but Demogorgon's concluding prophecy shatters the dream, confirming the repeated implication that we witness no more than reverie. In "The Witch of Atlas" the impermanence of the social reforms becomes evident in the evanescence of the Witch's communion with men. Indeed, the humorous, light hearted tone of "The Witch of Atlas" perfectly complements the frivolities by which the "lovely lady" tries to forget her isolation. Her relation with man is no more permanent than her relation with the nymphs and animals of stanzas 6 to 22. The tamed beasts, too limited for permanent communion, are tamed inadvertently; tamed only to be driven away. The Witch must remain alone because Shelley has not created for her a complementary being like Prometheus and because man cannot sustain his imaginative intimations of divinity. In "Prometheus Unbound," the aestheticism of the immortals parallels the dreamlike impermanence of man's imaginative awakening. This parallel prevents an unqualified affirmation and throws a shadow over the concluding festivities.

This shadow is skepticism both about man's ability to see phenomenal reality clearly and about his ability to maintain transcendent awareness. And again, as in his earlier work, Shelley has focused this skepticism in the mirror image. Fallen man is as "a many-sided mirror" ("Prometheus Unbound," 4.382–84) making metaphors into idols. The aestheticism of the united Asia and Prometheus mirrors man's dream-like existence on a revivified planet. While in act 4 this "dream" no longer involves idolatry, it still implies an inability to maintain imaginative perception (4.562–78). The dream of the "millennial men" is also the dream of the sleeping Spirit of the Earth, who both mocks and is mocked by "the orb's harmony" and who is himself mirrored in the infantile Hermaphrodite of "The Witch of Atlas." That poem in its entirety mirrors the salient tension of the last two acts: human imaginative limitation versus a Keatsian eternity of unfulfilled intimation.

The mirror is the ideal medium for Shelley's expression of skepticism, since it enables the mind, not only to see itself objectively in a dramatic context, but also to perceive, in a dramatically effective way, the limits of its own vision. The ironic tension of the last acts of "Prometheus Unbound" results both from the balancing of opposite perspectives through the mirrored perceptions and from the presentation of this process in a context of celebration.

For both poems celebrate life, even while acknowledging the limits of vision. When one turns from these works to "Adonais" and "The Triumph of Life," however, one discovers that the celebration has been totally silenced and that the limitations of human knowledge which were a source of irony in "Prometheus Unbound" and "The Witch of Atlas" have taken precedence over all other concerns.

5 THE OTHER SELF

"Adonais" and "The Triumph of Life"

THE poetic skepticism thus far considered focuses on the impossibility of knowing the noumenal ground of being and on the impossibility of either sustaining or adequately portraying intimation of the eternal Forms. These two aspects of Shelley's skepticism, roughly designated as "the empirical" and "the Platonic," engender very different attitudes to reform. "Alastor," "Mont Blanc," the Hymn, much of "The Revolt of Islam," and the first act of "Prometheus Unbound" are primarily concerned with "empirical" skepticism; they explore the positive effects of its social application and the negative effects of its eclipse by socially sanctioned dogma. However, in the latter half of "Prometheus Unbound" and in "The Witch of Atlas," Shelley's main thematic concern seems to shift; his main concern is not, as in earlier work, the social responsibility imposed by metaphysical skepticism, but, rather, the impossibility of sustaining, either in language or in life, intimation of transcendent reality. Finally, in his last major poems, "Adonais" and "The Triumph of Life," Shelley's awareness of this impossibility darkens his view of existence to a point where the earlier social concern seems supplanted by the desire for personal, or perhaps communal, transcendence.[1]

105

This shift in thematic balance is of course the primary theme of Ross Woodman's excellent study. Between Woodman and Wasserman, it would seem to me that the structure, development, and thematic implications of "Adonais" have been explored to a point where further exegesis requires very strong justification. My own justification for this chapter's additional remarks lies in the nature of my argument as a whole. I have shown that Shelley, in his earlier poetry, employed the *Doppelgänger* or mirror device to hold up to the mind either its own dogmatic lapses or its own perceptual inadequacy. There is indeed a sense in which Shelley's major poems themselves serve as mirrors of each other. The cavern-river-star image-sequence of "The Revolt of Islam" is ironically tempered by the descent, apotheosis, and anticlimactic reunion which occur in "Prometheus Unbound," and this sequence of episodes is in turn parodied by the Witch's playful progress from cave, over water, and through the skies. In "Adonais" and "The Triumph of Life," Shelley carries this mirroring process still further. Not only do these poems repeat the movement from cavern to stream to transcendence which, in one way or another, has already occurred in "The Revolt of Islam" and its poetic mirrors, including "Alastor" and "Mont Blanc," but, besides this, they make the image-pattern emphasize the limits of perception even more strongly. This skepticism calls into question the thematic validity of all the preceding poems, excepting perhaps the totally skeptical "Alastor." Since these last poems are, in a sense, mocking mirrors of Shelley's whole preceding career, then it is logical that, in them, the *Doppelgänger* device should be carried several steps further than previously, as indeed it is. In these last poems Shelley not only mirrors himself directly through poetic self-portrait, but also makes his objectified persona confront its alter ego—first, in Keats, and, second, in Rousseau.

Thus the *Doppelgänger* or mirroring device is employed, with increasing frequency and complexity, throughout Shelley's mature career. Indeed, it is fair to say that the better part of Shelley's poetic career consists in a continually shifting objectification and examination of his own mind. The mind is rendered dramatic to itself by the artist's constant probing of its objectifications; by his continual reassessment of the nature and significance of his own objectified thought processes. In his employment of this method, Shelley renders metaphysical skepticism a viable artistic theme which can be treated with exceptional particularity. This is, in my view, his most significant artistic achievement, and, in "Adonais" and "The Triumph of Life," that achievement is consummated. Each is a brilliant work in itself, but, when related to what precedes them, these poems resonate with an intellectual subtlety and scope rare in poetry or, for that matter, in any art.

This subtlety is best explored in two phases: in a consideration of how and why Keats and Rousseau provide alter egos for the poet's objectified consciousness, and in a consideration of the development of the imagery and thematic implications of the poems. In the case of "Adonais" this latter task has been so masterfully performed by Wasserman and Woodman, to name no others, that it would be pointless to attempt an examination of the imagery in its entirety. On the other hand, the imagistic development of "Triumph of Life" is so impressively particularized, both in detail and in implication, as to require a separate chapter; no one, in my view, has yet done it full justice.

First, then, a brief consideration of "Adonais." Paradoxically, this poem employs all the trappings of classical elegy in order to repudiate the validity of classical elegy and of all art as an expression of Eternity's "white radiance."[2] Despite the brilliance of Wasserman's study of "Adonais," I am personally puzzled by his reluctance to acknowledge that Shelley's concluding exhortation to the reader ("Die, / If thou wouldst be with that which thou dost seek!" [ll. 464–65]) is, in Woodman's phrase, "a metaphysical defence of suicide."[3] Shelley, after all, is very explicit here: life and all the things that go with it, including art ("ruins, statues, music" [l. 467]), constitute a "stain," blotting out the "white radiance" that may be fully attained only through transcendence of both life and art. Birth, as described by Shelley in stanza 54, is an "eclipsing Curse." The denotative meaning of this statement is too clear to be altered substantially by critical qualification, no matter how ingenious.[4] Whether or not death will actually bring transcendence is another question, but Shelley's repudiation of existence is hardly understated.[5]

Wasserman's study of the structural interrelation of stanzas 1 to 17 (esp. ll. 16–18, 48–54, 136–37), 18 to 37 (esp. ll. 158, 172–75), and 38 to 55 (esp. ll. 373–74, 440–41, 466–68, 478) admirably demonstrates how, in "Adonais," Shelley's imagination "dissolves, diffuses, and dissipates" environmental impressions, re-creating them into the monistic death world of section 1, the man-nature dualism of section 2, and the Platonic time-eternity antithesis of section 3. Since, in these last stanzas, it is the transcendence attained by Keats-Adonais which prompts Shelley's ultimate decision to transcend this world, the Keatsian echoes of stanzas 2 (cf. ll. 17–18 and "Isabella," stanza 54), 6 (cf. ll. 46–49 and "Isabella," stanza 54), 9 (cf. ll. 73–77 and "Ode to Psyche," ll. 5–6, 50–67), 17 (cf. ll. 145–49 and "Ode to a Nightingale," "On Seeing the Elgin Marbles," "Hyperion," ll. 224–28), 20 (cf. ll. 172–76 and "Isabella," stanza 54), 25 (cf. ll. 217–18 and "Ode On Melancholy," ll. 25–30), and 40 (cf. ll. 357–58 and "Ode to a Nightingale," stanza 3) are ultimately given a specifically Shelleyan significance. The echoes of Keats's poetry in "Adonais" transform that poetry's significance for the reader; viewed from Shelleyan perspective, Keats's poetry finally becomes a harbinger of eternity, or, to put it another way, Keats's poetic career comes to mirror Shelley's own.

When one turns from "Adonais" to the "Defence of Poetry," one discovers that this latter significance may be ascribed, not only to Keats's work, but to all great poetry, since the imaginative inspiration prompting poetic composition is as "the interpenetration of a diviner nature through our own."[6] Shelley warns, however, that since "the mind in creation is as a fading coal . . . the most glorious poetry that has ever been communicated to the world is probably only a feeble shadow of the original conception of the Poet."[7] Between the imaginative intimation of the divine Forms and the poetic embodiment of this intimation falls the shadow of the mortal world, with its "unwilling dross" ("Adonais," l. 384) of earthly images. Belonging as they do to the world of time, these images must be poetically "compelled" by the "plastic stress" of man's divine spirit; by the divinity within the mind which, in its ultimate identity with the transcendent One, is "One Spirit" ("Adonais," l. 381) "sweep[ing] through the dull, dense world" ("Adonais," l. 382) and remolding mortality's frozen impressions into imperfect images of eternity (ll. 384–85). Thus re-created, environmental images become harbingers of transcendence, "a record of [those] best and happiest moments" of man's divine intimation.[8] In order to awaken the reader to awareness of his own buried divinity, poetry "sends . . . forth" the "vanishing apparitions" of transcendent divinity "veil[ed] . . . in language." Thus poetry not only "redeems from decay the visitations of the divinity in man," but also awakens others to awareness of their transcendent origin and destiny.[9]

In "Adonais," Shelley's belief in the transcendent import of all inspired poetry enables him, without contradiction, both to emulate, as if in tribute, Keats's lamentations over mortality (especially stanzas 25 and 26) and to assert the transcendent significance of Keats's poetry. In the "Defence of Poetry," this same belief prompts Shelley's claim that "the distorted notions of invisible things which Dante and his rival Milton have idealised, are merely the mask and the mantle in which these great poets walk through eternity enveloped and disguised."[10] The religious beliefs Dante and Milton expressed through their poetry are, according to Shelley, merely part of that "unwilling dross" of earthly imagery which is utilized by the divinely inspired artist. Shelley suggests that such aesthetic refraction may indeed be necessary to "temper [the] planetary music" of transcendent intimation "to mortal ears,"[11] this latter process accounting partially for Christ's employment of parables.[12]

But while, in the *Commedia*, Dante's "heretical caprice in his distribution of rewards and punishments"[13] and, in *Paradise Lost*, Milton's heroic portrayal of Satan, both suggest—to Shelley at least—that these poets *consciously* tempered their divine inspiration to the cultural milieux of their times, it is also possible for a poet to express his transcendent intuitions while actually "denying" and "abjuring" the anagogic import of his own work.[14] Accordingly, whatever their personal convictions, "all poets" cooperate in producing, not a multitude of isolated works, but rather "one great poem," the imperfect image of Eternity.[15]

Once Shelley has reached this position, it logically follows that, on an anagogic level, all great poetic works become equally significant to him as harbingers of eternity. Accordingly, all genuine poets, whatever their differences in aesthetic, religious, or political persuasion, are essentially one. Thus, for Shelley, the reading of Keats, or indeed of any great poet, becomes the beholding of his own divine essence objectified in another man's words.

This is why, repeatedly in "Adonais," Keats is considered in the context of the entire poetic community, living and dead. In stanza 5, for example, there is undoubtedly a distinction among those poets who "knew" their own happiness through public recognition, those who died before their public reputation was consolidated (Keats's "refulgent prime" [l. 43]), and those who, though generally unrecognized, continue the attempt to illumine the minds of their contemporaries through poetry (surely Shelley is among these, ll. 44–45). Yet the concluding stanzas of the poem show these distinctions to be of minimal importance. The reason "Death can join" Shelley with Keats (l. 477) is not that death is the gateway to any *vitam venturi saeculi* (though it may be that), but, more significantly, that Keats and Shelley, as great poets, share the same divine essence. Thus, with life's superficial distinctions eliminated, they will be essentially one. The last stanza shows Shelley stripping off earthly disguises to join "the Eternal" (l. 495) who have, either consciously or unconsciously, heralded transcendence through their work (note the list of poetic luminaries in stanzas 45 and 46).

The inevitable question this position poses is the same confronted earlier in "The Revolt of Islam." If Laon and Cythna have the capacity for transcendent union, why do they concern themselves with earthly affairs? The answer, expressed in canto 9 of "The Revolt of Islam" (25–36), is that social revolutions, intially inspired by Cythna's skepticism, will lead ultimately to the millennium. Although, in "Prometheus Unbound," the permanence of man's millennial state seems disputable, the united gods' vicarious participation in human affairs improves life. Even the Witch of Atlas, in her desultory and detached fashion, grants mortals divine inspiration which effects temporary reform.

"Adonais," however, holds out no hope whatever of a coming millennium or even of any temporary change in man's condition. While the last two acts of "Prometheus Unbound" portray earthly life as a sleep, "Adonais" portrays it as a continual nightmare:

> Peace, peace! he is not dead, he doth but sleep—
> He hath awakened from the dream of life—
> 'Tis we, who lost in stormy visions, keep
> With phantoms an unprofitable strife,
> And in mad trance, strike with our spirit's knife
> Invulnerable nothings:—*We* decay
> Like corpses in a charnel; fear and grief
> Convulse us and consume us day by day,
> And cold hopes swarm like worms within our living clay.
> [39.343–51]

To the extent that earth is sustained by divinity, it is good; but matter is still, at best, an "unwilling dross" (l. 384), and divinity can manifest itself in matter only insofar "as each mass may bear" (l. 385). There is no suggestion anywhere in "Adonais" that the "unwilling dross" of matter can ever be transformed into a millennial paradise through man's imaginative awakening. Although "the dead live" (l. 395) when "lofty thought" (l. 392) lifts man to awareness of his divine essence, it must also be emphasized that the dead live in the imaginatively awakened man only because he realizes his essential identity with the great imaginers of every age. Nowhere in "Adonais" does Shelley suggest that such realization has any more than private significance; its tendency is toward individual transcendence rather than toward social reform. Indeed, the poem ends with Shelley himself scornfully ("trembling throng," l. 489) leaving phenomenal reality behind him.

Hence the skepticism imbuing the cave-water-star image-pattern takes on a darker cast than ever before. The cave image in earlier poetry (and in the prose) represented the human mind. In that cave are the "secret springs" ("Mont Blanc," l. 4) of human perception, a source which the poet of "Alastor" failed to discover ("Alastor," ll. 502–14), which "Mont Blanc" described as inaccessible, and which, in "The Revolt of Islam," was unknowable (8.4–9). This secret source of perception, however, engenders imaginative vision; it is the fountain in "the still cave of the witch Poesy" ("Mont Blanc," l. 44). In "Prometheus Unbound," both the Earth and Panthea describe a cavern whose oracular vapor prompts man to worship the icons of his own inaccessible life-source ("Prometheus Unbound," 2.3.1–10; 3.3.124–30). This negative portrayal of the cave image represents man's negative response to imaginative intuition. Just as Mont Blanc's inaccessible peak can produce both destructive glaciers (ll. 100–14) and nourishing streams (ll. 120–26), so the imaginative intuition of eternity can prompt either dogmatic idolatry or socially renovating skepticism. The latter, positive, response to imaginative vision is the issue of Asia's descent to the cave of shapeless Demogorgon (2.4). After having her skepticism confirmed ("The deep truth is imageless," 2.4.116), she travels imaginatively, like Laon and Cythna, by water and by air (2.4.129–74; 2.5), finally reuniting with Prometheus.

At this point, however, "Prometheus Unbound" reintroduces the cave image, this time to delineate the poem's essential difference from "The Revolt of Islam." Whereas Laon and Cythna were reunited *in* a temple which symbolized transcendent reality, Prometheus and Asia spend the time of their reunion *beside* a temple—*in* a cave. This once-volcanic cave, formerly sufficiently active to lure "the . . . nations round to mutual war" (hence symbolizing imaginative intuition to which man responds negatively [3.3.129]), is now a paradisal shelter whence the united couple learn of earthly vicissitudes (3.3.10–63). The temple beside it, however, still remains a symbol of transcendent reality. The temples of both "The Revolt of Islam" and "Prometheus Unbound" are recalled in the allusion to "the inmost veil of Heaven" (l. 493) which concludes Shelley's own aerial voyage in "Adonais." But if the temple allusion has the same significance in all three poems, what can be said of the cave allusion?

In "Prometheus Unbound," the cave allusion of act 3 is anticlimactic. Specifically what the cave of act 3 symbolizes is difficult to say, but it certainly restores infantile innocence to its inhabitants, and their placid, if not apathetic, state is paralleled and intensified in that of the cave-born Witch of Atlas. I think both caves are indeed caves of "the witch Poesy," but these poems view the witch Poesy in a very severe light. Taken in its entirety, Shelley's verse provides many different commentaries on W. H. Auden's claim that "poetry makes nothing happen."[16] Clearly poetry *can* make things happen in "Mont Blanc" and "The Revolt of Islam"; in the latter, poetic inspiration assures the millennium. But in "Prometheus Unbound" imaginative vision accomplishes considerably less, and this shrinking of the imagination's social and political scope is carried farther in "The Witch of Atlas." In both poems the mind-cave of the revolutionary imagination threatens to become the womb-cave of passive aestheticism. By the time of "Adonais," however, the cave has been transformed to a virtual tomb.

The image of the poet's mind as tomb is a central unifying motif in "Adonais." In stanza 7 the tomb image is introduced directly with the description of Keats's resting place in Rome. By stanza 9, however, the tomb image has been internalized: Keats's mind is, by implication, a dried-up fountainhead. It thus provides a parallel (though much altered) with the "secret springs" in the living mind-cave of "the witch Poesy" ("Mont Blanc," ll. 4, 44), or with the fountains in the sheltering caves of "Prometheus Unbound" (3.3.10–14) and "The Witch of Atlas" (ll. 55–56, 241–42). Now that Adonais is deceased he can no longer feed (l. 76) his poetic visions with inspiration. The mind's Hippocrene has dried and, accordingly, the "living streams" (l. 75, cf. "Alastor," ll. 502–14; "Mont Blanc," ll. 1–11, 120–26; "The Revolt of Islam," 9.35–36, 12.33–41; "Prometheus Unbound," 2.5.72–110; "The Witch of Atlas," 35, 38 ff.) of poetic vision can no longer awaken others. Although Keats's mind is never explicitly described as cave or tomb, it is nevertheless his own dreams which, metaphorically, embalm and memorialize him (11–12), and, by the logic of the text, the procession of stanza 13 visits the dead cave of Keats's mind, rather than his external monument: the visitors are, after all, mind-born entities (also 14.118–20). Indeed, the primary significance of the extension of the list of mourners to include not merely Keats's own imaginative creations, but also the environmental elements (14–16), is surely that the objects of Keats's perception have faded with his perception itself. Thus the "woe" of the transitional eighteenth stanza results, not merely from Shelley's realization that the seasonal cycle continues despite Keats's death, but also from awareness that "external reality" is not dependent upon human perception. Shelley suggests as much in stanza 20, where he moves from the initial emphasis on individual perception (cf. "Alastor," ll. 502–14) to a restatement of the mind-object interdependence already articulated in the one mind concept of "On Life" and "Mont Blanc":

> Nought we know, dies. Shall that alone which knows
> Be . . . consumed?
>
> [Ll. 176–77]

Shelley's question, however, takes us a step farther toward a "common sense" epistemology than did "Mont Blanc." If "that alone which knows" were all that were "consumed," then the objects of perception could exist independently. Shelley, in his skepticism, is considering all possibilities.

It will be clear from these comments that I read "Adonais" "straight." I do not discount the statements of the first two-thirds of the poem as rhetorical gestures, merely preparing the way for the concluding affirmation. The revelation the last stanzas present is a shift of perspective made possible by the speaker's imminent death, and the device of addressing us in this circumstance enables Shelley, or his persona, to undercut his vision with characteristic skepticism. To appreciate the skepticism, however, one must assume that the author, at all times, means what he says. This is by no means an unusual critical attitude, even toward pastoral elegy. One does not assume, at the conclusion of "Lycidas," that Milton really intends to herd sheep. One does assume that he intends to get back to the business of living. One does not assume, at the conclusion of "Adonais," that Shelley is actually voyaging to a transcendent reality. One does assume that he regards such a voyage as the only way to happiness or certainty.

The metaphorical and imagistic development of the poem is rooted in a continuous shift of philosophical perspective. The skepticism which formerly had prompted Shelley to modify and redefine his symbols from poem to poem, and, in "Prometheus Unbound," from act to act, now prompts him to modify and redefine his images from stanza to stanza within the poem itself. At first, the death of Keats's imaginative perception seems to precipitate the death of perceptual objects. Then, in stanza 18, comes the emphatic declaration that "nought we know, dies"—an abrupt philosophical modulation. But skepticism remains about the fate of the knower and, in stanza 21, this skepticism intensifies. Can we indeed "know" the external world?

> Whence are we, and why are we? of what scene
> The actors or spectators?
>
> [Ll. 183–84]

At this point the cave image, implicitly at least, re-enters the poem.

The image is re-introduced through the reference to Urania (22) who, whatever her symbolic significance, is definitely presented as the Muse and the spiritual bride of Milton. Keats was the "youngest" and "dearest" (l. 46) of her spiritual offspring, the "nursling" of Urania's "widowhood" (l. 47). The implication, of course, is that Keats was Milton's poetic heir and, accordingly, Urania was the source of his poetic inspiration. This is obvious enough, but, once one has accepted it, the question of stanza 2 introduces considerably more than a Bionic echo:

> Where wert thou, mighty Mother, when he lay,
> When thy Son lay, pierced by the shaft which flies
> In darkness? where was lorn Urania
> When Adonais died?
>
> [Ll. 20–23]

The "shaft" is the adverse criticism which Shelley believed to have caused Keats's death, but the question, given its context, can be paraphrased, with adequate accuracy, as follows: Where was Keats's imaginative strength when earthly corruption threatened his existence? Where, in other words, was the source of his imaginative insight—the power which could have countered, or at least opposed, slander and injustice?

While the answer to this question is dismaying, it is hardly surprising in the light of what has already transpired in both "Prometheus Unbound" and "The Witch of Atlas." Urania, as muse, was the source of Keats's imaginative power. At the time of his demise

> With veilèd eyes
> 'Mid listening Echoes, in her Paradise
> She sate, while one, with soft enamoured breath,
> Rekindled all the fading melodies,
> With which, like flowers that mock the corse beneath,
> He had adorned and hid the coming bulk of Death.
>
> [Ll. 13–18]

Flowers indeed "mock" the corpse, by hiding the reality of corruption. But the flowers here are Keats's own poems ("He," l. 18) and Urania, rather than opposing both physical and moral corruption, sits in her sheltered paradise, while one of her attendants sings to her. The parallels are obvious:

> We will sit and talk of time and change,
> As the world ebbs and flows, ourselves unchanged.
> What can hide man from mutability?
> And if ye sigh, then I will smile; and thou,
> Ione, shalt chant fragments of sea-music,
> Until I weep, when ye shall smile away
> The tears she brought, which yet were sweet to shed.
>
> ["Prometheus Unbound," 3.3.23–29]

> And on a throne o'erlaid with starlight, caught
> Upon those wandering isles of aëry dew
> Which highest shoals of mountain shipwreck not,
> She sate, and heard all that had happened new
> Between the earth and moon, since they had brought
> The last intelligence—and now she grew
> Pale as that moon, lost in the watery night—
> And now she wept, and now she laughed outright.
>
> ["The Witch of Atlas," 54]

These passages, both through their tone and through the symbolic significance of their characters, cast doubt on the efficacy of imaginative power in bringing the "ebb and flow" of social struggle to a permanent and positive conclusion. All three passages are couched in a deliberately languid tone, delineating the limitations, not merely of aestheticism, but of imagination itself. This inadequacy is the primary point of Urania's theatrical lament in stanzas 25 to 29. Her suggestion that Keats could have effectively opposed calumny had he waited until his maturity before entering the public arena (27) is directly belied by the fate of her "husband," Milton (4). Moreover, just as Bion's Aphrodite wished to follow Adonis to Acheron, so Urania wishes to join Keats in death. But, since she is "chained to Time" (l. 234), she cannot. Thus she is, as it were, "in the world but not of it." Like the Witch of Atlas, or like the united Asia and Prometheus, she seems suspended between mortality and eternity, with little capacity (or, perhaps inclination) for effecting permanent social amelioration.

As bride of the author of *Paradise Lost*, Urania inhabits a "Paradise" (l. 14) from which she arises "swift as a Thought by the snake Memory stung" (l. 197). This becomes particularly significant when one considers that the mind of the dead Keats is similarly described as "a ruined Paradise" (l. 88) and that his own "fading melodies" (l. 16) pervade Urania's paradisal dreamworld. These "melodies" are the equivalent of Prometheus's "sea-music" (3.3.27). Implicitly at least, the use and validity of imaginative writing are being severely questioned.

To this extent, then, the mind-cave symbolism has been both maintained and modified, providing a skeptical parody both of its own earlier occurrences and of Shelley's own mind at the time of writing. For if, as the poem implies, poetic inspiration is both time-bound and socially ineffectual, then Shelley, as poet, is indeed, in a very literal sense, lamenting "his own" lot in weeping for Adonais (l. 300).

That very lament, in the latter stanzas of the poem, prompts Shelley's assertion that artistic endeavor distorts transcendent divinity ("Flowers, ruins, statues, music, words, are weak / The glory they transfuse with fitting truth to speak" [ll. 468–69]). This realization, in turn, directs his own vision beyond time, rendering him a stranger to the time-bound Urania (l. 303). The voyage to transcendent reality which had been previously granted Laon, Cythna, and Asia is now undertaken by Shelley's own persona. The difference, however, between this voyage and the earlier voyages, is that *they* were prompted by a descent to the "secret springs" of inspiration, whereas this voyage begins in a cemetery (51–54) and is less a fulfillment of imaginative intimation than an escape from the living mind's inadequacy (note, for example, the "pursuit" of stanza 31 and the reference to flight in line 466). As "phantom" (l. 272), fugitive (ll. 278–79), and "dying lamp" (l. 284), Shelley's persona finds its alter ego in a corpse, thus verifying literally the Earth's claim that "Death is the veil which those who live call life" ("Prometheus Unbound," 3.3.113). To the extent that it is "a Love in desolation masked;—a Power / Girt round with weakness" (ll. 281–82), Shelley's persona still contains within itself the divine nucleus or "prototype" that will find in transcendent reality its complement.

But can one be sure that one's intimations of divinity are trustworthy, especially considering that Urania herself, symbol of poetic inspiration, is "chained to Time?" Through skepticism and self-objectification "Adonais" casts doubt upon the validity of all courses of action except flight. With "The Triumph of Life" Shelley takes the next logical step on his journey back to the total skepticism of "Alastor," since in his last poem flight itself is repudiated and all possibilities of knowledge are called into question.

The point of Shelley's self-portrait and of the choice of the dead Keats as alter ego (I say "the dead Keats" because Shelley's persona laments his *own* fate in weeping over the corpse [l. 300]) will be clear from this brief consideration of "Adonais." However, there are also significant biographical reasons for Shelley's choice of Keats as alter ego. Surely the urge for self-justification was a central motive for Shelley's poetic defense of the deceased poet. Some of the passages omitted from the preface to "Adonais" raise doubt whether Shelley's primary motive in writing the poem was the celebration of Keats or the vindication of himself: "Persecution, contumely, and calumny have been heaped upon me in profuse measure; and domestic conspiracy and legal oppression have violated in my person the most sacred rights of nature and humanity."[17] The indignant tone, although perhaps biographically justified, becomes, as many have observed, excessive in Shelley's self-portrait ("a herd-abandoned deer struck by the hunter's dart" [l. 297]).[18] Here Shelley is certainly paralleling himself with Keats, who has been struck by the "shaft" of anonymous critical censure.

Thus the mirror motif recurs again. Shelley sees Keats as his alter ego because he regards both Keats and himself as victims of unjustified attack. Indeed, the "woe is me" of line 155 emphasizes Shelley's grief more than Keats's misfortune, as does the self-portrait, the reference to young William (51), and the bitter repudiation of "man," "woman," and all else which "crushes" and "withers" the victimized author (53). Clearly Keats's career presented to Shelley a scandalous instance of the social persecution of neglected genius. Since he regarded himself as both persecuted and neglected, it was inevitable that, in memorializing Keats, Shelley should also lament his own lot. If this were the only significance of his lament, however; if the lament were not ultimately rooted in a heightened skepticism about both the social and personal value of imaginative expression, then the poem would lose much in subtlety and depth.

The same may be said of Shelley's choice of Rousseau as alter ego in "The Triumph of Life." I have no doubt that Rousseau presents Shelley with a mirror of his own experience, but I will delay most of my arguments on this point until the next chapter. The most significant reason that Rousseau holds up to Shelley his own image is that, despite some reservations, Shelley had high respect for Rousseau both as a thinker and as an artist.[19] Accordingly, Rousseau is among those imaginers whose work refracts Eternity's white light, and the anagogic import of his work is the same as that of Keats or Shelley: it shows that the attainment and expression of transcendent awareness are, socially, ineffectual in prompting sustained reform and, individually, a distortion of essential reality into existential illusion.

That Shelley saw in Rousseau's *La Nouvelle Heloise* both an adumbration and distortion of transcendent divinity is clear as early as 1816. Shelley discerned in Rousseau's novel a prefiguration of transcendence quite out of keeping with the latter's worship of nature as the handiwork of God.[20] Suitably enough, Shelley was prompted to comment on Rousseau by his own perception of the natural scenery described in *La Nouvelle Heloise*. Touring the environs of Geneva in 1816, Shelley wrote:

> It is nearly a fortnight since I have returned from Vevai. This journey has been on every account delightful, but most especially, because then I first knew the divine beauty of Rousseau's imagination, as it exhibits itself in Julie. It is inconceivable what an enchantment the scene itself lends to those delineations, from which its own most touching charm arises.

And further:

> I read Julie all day; an overflowing, as it now seems, surrounded by the scenes which it has so wonderfully peopled, of sublimest genius, and more than human sensibility. Meillerie, the Castle of Chillon, Clarens, the mountains of La Valais and Savoy, present themselves to the imagination as monuments of things that were once familiar, and of beings that were once dear to it. They were created indeed by one mind, but a mind so powerfully bright as to cast a shade of falsehood on the records that are called reality.[21]

If Keats made "the loveliness" of nature "more lovely" ("Adonais," ll. 379–80) by dissipating and re-creating its impressions in his poetry, Shelley's perception of "the scene" described in Rousseau's *Julie* gave an added "enchantment" to Rousseau's description, and vice versa. In "Adonais," art's heralding of transcendence through re-created natural impressions makes one perceive nature itself with renewed imaginative power. Hence the intimation of Adonais's voice through the perception of natural images in stanza 53. This interrelation of art and mind brings about the transcendence of stanza 55. Similarly in the above passages the perceptual interrelation of the natural scenery with its descriptions in *La Nouvelle Heloise* intensifies the imaginative awareness of the divinity lying behind both. Inasmuch as the divinity in Rousseau's mind is ultimately identical with the divinity of the transcendent realm, the scenery he described and his description itself are alike creations of "one mind." The "one mind" to which Shelley refers, however, is not the mind which consciously reasons, but the divine spirit which man inherits from Eternity. Thus Shelley, writing in 1816, attempts to qualify his metaphorical use of the term *mind*. He asserts that both the natural scene and the writing of Rousseau "were created . . . by . . . a mind so powerfully bright as to cast a shade of falsehood on the records that are called reality." This sentence not only suggests that by *mind* Shelley means the transcendent divinity, but also qualifies his earlier use of the word *create*. The divinity in the mind creates poetry only insofar as it is itself the Splendor which poetry shadows forth, while the divinity of the Forms creates the natural world only insofar as the latter is the former's imperfect reflection. Moreover, in employing earthly images to record transcendent intimations, "the records that are called reality" almost falsify the divinity they shadow forth. Between 1816 and 1822 Shelley's dissatisfaction with this "falsification" became unbearable.

But this dichotomy between nature on the one hand and transcendent reality on the other is something quite foreign to Rousseau, at least as he is understood by the non-Shelleyan. *La Nouvelle Heloïse* itself concerns the pursuit of spiritual perfection *on this earth*, with nature often envisaged as Eden, fresh from the hand of God, and Julie's marriage to Wolmar—rather than to Saint-Preux—prompting an unprecedented richness in her religious life and culminating in her dying "profession of faith."[22] The novel's hero, Saint-Preux, through his purgatorial experiences with his pious beloved, Julie, finally achieves a serenity born of self-mastery and of fellowship in Julie's society of "spiritually pure" individuals.[23] The book is in part a dramatization of Rousseau's understanding of his own religious development, and that development at no point involves the deprecatory view of this world as a "clog" on man's divinity, or of life as a "stain" blotting a transcendent Unity.[24]

Nevertheless, Shelley's comments on the novel indicate that he read it from the perspective of his own Orphic Platonism. Thus Rousseau's work, like that of Keats in "Adonais," is accommodated to Shelley's own philosophical framework. When Shelley's dissatisfaction with art's falsification is consummated, Rousseau joins those other brilliant imaginers whose efforts merely decorate life's refractive and distorting "many-coloured glass." Thus, in "The Triumph of Life," referring both to his own work and to that of other intellectual luminaries, Rousseau says:

> "Figures ever new
> Rise on the bubble, paint them how you may;
> We have but thrown, as those before us threw,
>
> Our shadows on it as it past away."[25]

The "bubble" has already been defined by Shelley as the world's "false & fragile glass" (ll. 244–47). But, although this dome of many-colored glass has, for Rousseau, already "past away," he has not achieved transcendence; instead, he exists in a sort of limbo, as Virgilian shade presenting life's inferno to Shelley. Transcendent reality is the "native noon" (l. 131) to which Socrates and Christ return (ll. 128–35), but the majority of the dead evidently do not "cross over," and one is accordingly left in doubt whether even the flight with which "Adonais" concludes can free one from illusion. I will develop this idea in the next chapter.

Rousseau also comments on his own career in language strongly reminiscent of Coleridge's comparison between Luther and Rousseau in *The Friend*. There is now convincing evidence that Shelley was familiar with Coleridge's criticism of Rousseau's personality and political philosophy.[26] Coleridge saw Rousseau as a man possibly possessing the sensibility and intellectual powers of Luther, but born in a time when there was no great object upon which these powers could be exercised.[27] If one bears in mind that Shelley, in all probability, knew of Coleridge's comments, Rousseau's self-characterization in "The Triumph of Life" can be seen as an echo of Coleridge's observations, or, at least, as an endorsement of Coleridge's opinion. Rousseau speaks to Shelley:

> "Before thy memory,
>
> I feared, loved, hated, suffered, did & died,
> *And if the spark with which Heaven lit my spirit*
> *Earth had with purer nutriment supplied*
>
> Corruption would not now thus much inherit
> Of what was once Rousseau."
>
> [Ll. 199–204, my italics]

And further:

> "I was overcome
> By my own heart alone, which neither age
>
> Nor tears nor infamy nor now the tomb
> Could temper to its object."
>
> [Ll. 240–43]

To temper is either to moderate, as in tempering justice with mercy, or, as with clay or metal, to harden, soften, or in some way render usable.[28] The import of the passage is that Rousseau's temperament, sensibility, passions, and ideals were impervious to both decay and persecution (to both moral and natural "corruption"), yet, at the same time, were too great for the world in which he existed. Shelley did not like *The Confessions*, but, as "Adonais" shows, he was possessed of the same passion for self-justification which must have inspired *The Confessions*, and he certainly saw himself, too, as a persecuted man whose genius was largely unrecognized.[29] Hence the choice of Rousseau as alter ego.

Returning to *The Friend*: Coleridge is particularly interested in *The Social Contract*'s distinction between general will (*volonté générale*) and majority rule (*volonté de tous*). While the latter, as Rousseau admits, may reflect prejudicial self-interest, the former, springing directly from conscience and reason, provides an unerring guide for political policy. And, once the error of prejudicial self-interest has been eliminated through the mutual refutations of democratic debate, the general will emerges as the irrefutable basis for public authority.[30] Coleridge regarded this argument as utopian, especially in the light of the fanaticism and terror which characterized French politics after the revolution. He did not believe the general will could emerge triumphant from the unfettered political expression of public interest and opinion. Whether or not it was utopian, there is no doubt that, as Coleridge claims, the argument was susceptible of exploitation. Napolean, on assuming state control, justified his actions by an appeal to the general will, thus distorting Rousseau's democratic arguments into a pretext for despotism.[31]

In this light, Rousseau's proud assertion that "a thousand beacons [rise] from the spark I bore" (l. 207) emerges as Shelley's acknowledgment that right-minded people continue to interpret Rousseau's political theory in the humanitarian spirit which inspired it. Overbalancing this optimistic attitude, however, is the vision of the fallen Napoleon. Shelley's perspective on Napoleon reflects the disdain which, in Coleridge's view, Rousseau would have held for France's distortion of democratic political theory into a rationalization for tyranny:[32]

> I felt my cheek
> Alter to see the great form pass away
> Whose grasp had left the giant world so weak
>
> That every pigmy kicked it as it lay—
> And much I grieved to think how power & will
> In opposition rule our mortal day—
>
> And why God made irreconcilable
> Good and the means of good; and for *despair*
> I half disdained mine eye's desire to fill
>
> With the spent vision of the times that were
> And scarce have ceased to be.
>
> [Ll. 224–34, my italics]

This despair at the perversion of good intentions to bad ends is expressed quite explicitly by Rousseau himself:

> "I
> Am one of those who have created, even
> If it be but a world of agony."
>
> [Ll. 293–95]

Rousseau's "words were seeds of misery" (l. 280) not only because he "suffered what [he] wrote" (l. 279) but also because, through the misapplication of this theory, his writings increased, rather than diminished, the misery of man.[33]

This entire process repeats and personalizes the *Doppelgänger* mirroring of dogmatic tyranny which occurs in the first act of "Prometheus Unbound." The Furies present to Prometheus the mirror of his own dilemma. Just as his humanitarian opposition of Jupiter's tyranny has frozen the universe into a state of inhuman hatred, so the reforming efforts of both Christ and the French revolutionaries have prompted only a renewal of dogmatism. If, in "The Triumph of Life," the distortion of Rousseau's words prompts

Shelley to lament that "power & will / In opposition rule our mortal day" and that "God made irreconcilable / Good and the means of good," so, in "Prometheus Unbound":

> The good want power, but to weep barren tears.
> The powerful goodness want: worse need for them.
> The wise want love; and those who love want wisdom;
> *And all best things are thus confused to ill.*
>
> [Ll.625–28, my italics]

While, in "Prometheus Unbound," this skepticism about the efficacy of revolution is expressed through the *Doppelgänger* interrelation of figures from Greek mythology and characters from European history, "The Triumph of Life" intensifies the skepticism by mirroring the distortion of democratic idealism into tyrannical idolatry through the implied parallel between the careers of Shelley and Rousseau. For if, in the French Revolution and the history of the Christian Church, Prometheus sees, as in a mirror, the distortion of his own revolutionary efforts into renewed dogmatism, so Shelley, in the misapplication of Rousseau's ideas, sees, as in a mirror, the ineffectuality of his own reforming efforts.[34] One need only examine the bitter sonnet, "England in 1819," to realize that Shelley regarded his own country as deaf to the appeals of its reformers, including himself. In that poem, he hopes for the rise of "a glorious Phantom" to "illumine" his country's "tempestuous day," but, on the evidence of "The Triumph of Life," such an eventuality would appear most unlikely. Thus the choice of Rousseau as alter ego serves to personalize and intensify the poetic portrayal of mental and moral lethargy which, both in "Prometheus Unbound" and throughout Shelley's career, is the greatest enemy of revolutionary skepticism. It also emphasizes Shelley's own heightened skepticism about the efficacy of appeals to reason and humanity in the combat against tyranny.

But this very skepticism is itself a reflection of the antisocial, if not antiintellectual, strain that pervades much of Rousseau's writing. As early as 1815, Shelley had expressed interest in Rousseau's First Discourse, a work which attempts to prove that the development of the arts and sciences has consolidated, rather than lessened, tyranny and injustice.[35] Although references to Shelley's reading of *Émile* cannot be found before 1816,[36] and although there is nowhere in his poetry a portrayal of education which systematically reflects that work's precepts, Shelley neverthelesss devotes considerable space to the description of his heroes' intellectual development, and that development is usually portrayed as occurring in a state of nature[37] ("Alastor," ll. 67–106; "The Revolt of Islam," e.g., 2.5–15; "The Triumph of Life," ll. 296–97, 395 ff.) and is related, not to accepted social conventions, but to the individual's own emotional experience and needs in a solitary, natural state ("Alastor," ll. 75–128; "Mont Blanc," ll. 76–83; "Hymn to Intellectual Beauty," 5–7; "The Revolt of Islam," Dedication, 3–5; 1.38). There is of course as much of Wordsworth as of Rousseau in this theme, and it is thus hardly surprising that, in "The Triumph of Life," Wordsworth's Immortality Ode—essentially a description of man's education by nature—underlies Rousseau's description of his own development from infancy to manhood. In the next chapter I will explore that element in the poem and attempt to show how the poem itself denies the value of art. Since Rousseau was himself an artist who condemned the development of the arts, Shelley could hardly have chosen a better agent for the process of self-objectification and self-repudiation which occurs in his last great achievement.

6 APOCALYPTIC SKEPTICISM

"The Triumph of Life"

"THE Triumph of Life" is the poetic portrayal of total Humean skepticism. The poem not only raises a profusion of unanswered philosophical questions, but, more important, raises the tantalizing Humean issue: are answers possible? "The Triumph of Life" focuses this issue primarily through the protean metamorphoses of its images. For example: the shape all light does not stand *above* life's many-colored dome, but rather merges with it, moving on the stream and creating, from her light and water, the rainbow which pavilions the car of Life. Similarly, *both* the shape all light and the morning star with which she is compared follow the sun's diurnal cycle (ll. 416–32). The implication of finality in the seasonal images is dispelled by their juxtaposition with each other. Implications of religious or philosophical certainty in Shelley's rising sun are also dispelled by the sun's obedience to the diurnal cycle. Likewise, the apparently supernatural and thus, possibly, millennial dawn which begins Rousseau's vision gives way to the day's cycle of hours. Moreover, the reality of the "native noon" to which Socrates and Christ escape is itself, like the "true Sun" of Rousseau's narrative, called into question by the impermanence of the various supersolar lights. The rivers of Rousseau's vision flow

127

neither to an eternal sea nor to a land where there is no more sea, but instead are transformed into the stream of Life's wretched captives. The beginning and end of life's thronged highway remain unknown, if indeed existent. While, in "Mont Blanc," the Power underlying existence, although unknown, was nevertheless "there" (l. 127), "The Triumph of Life" seems to return to the severe skepticism of "Alastor": one wonders if there is, in fact, any source or conclusion for the life portrayed in the circling images. The failure of any of the many lights to disengage itself from earthly flux eliminates the possibility of an eternal "white radiance," just as the lights themselves render an eternal night impossible (see "Adonais," ll. 252–56).

The poem systematically posits image after image as potential analogue of ultimate reality and then, by submerging these images in life's natural cycle, poetically demonstrates their inadequacy. This strategy is the obverse of that followed in "Adonais," where the apparently death-bound analogues of the opening section (1–17, 18–37) are anagogically glossed in the conclusion (38–55).[1] The conclusion of "Adonais," however, with its revelation that the earlier images of lamentation have heralded transcendence, contains the root of its own destruction, since the implied equivalence of all the images as analogues of eternity threatens to shift attention from the eternity the images supposedly reflect to the inadequacy of the images themselves. This is in fact what occurs in "The Triumph of Life": a reversed apocalypse in which static images of eternity are submerged one by one in the natural cycle they should either encompass or supersede. Once this process has been completed, the poem has, in effect, repudiated both itself and all other poetry as harbinger of eternity.[2] Thus Shelley's poetic skepticism achieves its fullest expression and "The Triumph of Life" emerges as the palinode to his poetic career.[3]

Although many able critics have provided valuable explications of "The Triumph of Life,"[4] much remains to be said on the ingenious, self-destructive pattern of its imagery.[5] Whatever Shelley may have intended to add to this powerful fragment, its images form a complete cycle, beginning with a sunrise, concluding with a reference to the day's·decline (ll. 537–38), and presenting the image of noon as analogue of the eternity to which the "sacred few" (l. 128) who elude life's illusions return. Although the extent of life's dominion has been questioned,[6] one may say with assurance that the sacred few who escape life include at least Christ and Socrates (ll. 134–35), as well perhaps as some of their followers, and that the "native noon" (l. 131), defined in whatever terms, is an image of the abiding reality beyond life's cyclic flux.[7] At first sight the clear light of noon would, like "the white radiance of Eternity" ("Adonais," l. 463), seem a valid analogue for this transcendent realm. But the rest of the poem, intentionally I think, undermines this metaphor, and the "native noon" reference ultimately proves ironic, whether one relates it to the sunlight with which Shelley's and Rousseau's visions commence, to the shape all light, the appearance of which climaxes the poem, or to the matrix of darkness out of which the poem arises and into which it finally returns.

The "native noon" image bears an especially ironic relation to Shelley's opening portrayal of the sun. These twenty lines weld clarity of image and richness of implication: the eye takes in a single vision, through which the mind perceives a world of contraries. The union of the One and the Many may be impossible, but this remarkable passage, with its singleness of vision and its multitude of implications, certainly unifies the mind and eye:

> Swift as a spirit hastening to his task
> Of glory & of good, the Sun sprang forth
> Rejoicing in his splendour, & the mask
>
> Of darkness fell from the awakened Earth.
> The smokeless altars of the mountain snows
> Flamed above crimson clouds, & at the birth
>
> Of light, the Ocean's orison arose
> To which the birds tempered their matin lay.
> All flowers in field or forest which unclose
>
> Their trembling eyelids to the kiss of day,
> Swinging their censers in the element,
> With orient incense lit by the new ray
>
> Burned slow & inconsumably, & sent
> Their odorous sighs up to the smiling air,
> And in succession due, did Continent,

> Isle, Ocean, & all things that in them wear
> The form & character of mortal mould
> Rise as the Sun their father rose, to bear
>
> Their portion of the toil which he of old
> Took as his own & then imposed on them.[8]

The first three lines strongly echo the Nineteenth Psalm of David, and it has also been observed that the whole passage bears a close affinity with the following lines from Shelley's "The Boat on the Serchio"[9] which, whether ironic or orthodox in intent, posits the existence of a deity, however limited, and makes the sun, as in David's Nineteenth Psalm, a minister of that deity:[10]

> Day had kindled the dewy woods,
> And the rocks above and the stream below,
> And the vapours in their multitudes,
> And the Appenine's shroud of summer snow,
> . . . .
> Night's dreams and terrors, every one,
> Fled from the brains which are their prey
> From the lamp's death to the morning ray.
>
> All rose to do the task He set to each,
> Who shaped us to His ends and not our own.
>
> [Ll. 12–31]

In "The Triumph of Life," "the smokeless altars of the mountain snows" (l. 5) also bring to mind the snowy peak of Mont Blanc which, if not an altar, is still the dwelling place of a noumenal "Power" ("Mont Blanc," ll. 127, 139–41). Finally, and most significantly, the quoted passage unmistakably echoes stanza 43 of "Adonais":

> He is a portion of the loveliness
> Which once he made more lovely; he doth bear
> His part, while the one Spirit's plastic stress
> Sweeps through the dull dense world, compelling there,
> All new successions to the forms they wear;
> Torturing th' unwilling dross that checks its flight
> To its own likeness, as each mass may bear;
> And bursting in its beauty and its might
> From trees and beasts and men into the Heaven's light.
>
> [Ll. 379–87]

The spiritlike sun of "The Triumph of Life" and the "one Spirit" of "Adonais" fulfill very similar roles.[11] Since, in "The Triumph of Life," the sun is like "a spirit hastening to his task / Of glory and of good," his own task must have some anagogic equivalent. In lines 16 to 19 one learns that "all things that in them wear / The form and character of mortal mould / . . . bear / Their portion of the [sun's] toil." Similarly, Adonais, as "a portion of the loveliness / Which once he made more lovely" (ll. 379–80—i.e., as a part of eternity adumbrated in nature), "doth bear his part" in the "one Spirit's" compulsion of natural objects into its own "likeness" (ll. 380–85). Just as, from a natural perspective, the sun makes earthly objects "burn" (ll. 5–6, 11–14), "awake" (ll. 9–10), and "rise" (l. 18), thus rendering them imperfect mirrors of himself, so, from a transcendent perspective, the "one Spirit" compels earthly objects to mirror its divinity. When imaginatively perceived, "trees and beasts and men" ("Adonais," l. 387) reveal the immanence of that shaping spirit, and imaginative perception can transform natural objects into its emblems. Through such imaginative perception the sun of lines 1 to 20 could have become "the white radiance of Eternity," while the flowers and vaporous incense of lines 9 to 14 could, as in "Adonais," have become stars ("Adonais," ll. 390, 441, 478) and splendor ("Adonais," ll. 120–23, 362–63, 388–92), emblematizing eternity.[12] Shelley's comparison of the sun to a spirit and his portrayal of the flowers as earthly flames (ll. 13–15) indicate his awareness of this possibility. Nevertheless, his comparison remains mere comparison, similes prevailing in this Dantesque poem, and the natural scene is not metaphorically transformed.[13]

Still, the potentiality of the transcendent perspective is sufficiently evident to prompt recollection of the startling conclusion of "Adonais." Recalling that poem's progressive revelation, one might well expect the rising sun eventually to give way to eternity ("Adonais," l. 463) and the forest flowers to become "the immortal stars" ("Adonais," l. 256). To do so, however, would be to ignore the biblical and liturgical echoes in the description of the sun and in the natural imagery of the passage as a whole. The sun resembles a spirit not only by recalling the one Spirit's transcendental labors but also by fulfilling the functions of a paternal deity. Thus the mountains burn as altars at his rising; the ocean praises him, harmonizing its "orison" (l. 7) with the birds' "matin lay" (l. 8). Similarly the worshipping flowers swing their censers (l. 11), and the sun lights their "orient incense" (l. 12), making "Heaven and Earth . . . full of His glory." Ultimately, though, the sun is himself part of this worship (ll. 17–19)—a high priest presiding at a ritual. The toil which the sun took unto himself (l. 19) is that of regulating the natural cycle, and the natural cycle itself is by implication, here as in "The Boat on the Serchio" or in Psalm Nineteen, a ritual of praise to a divine Creator.[14] From this perspective, the anagoge of the sun is not the "one Spirit" of "Adonais" but "the sun that never sets," the pun of line 18 faintly echoing the liturgy of the Roman Catholic church ("Filium Dei unigenitum . . . consubstantialem Patri, per quem omnia facta sunt"). If the pun is unintentional, its aptness amid a milieu of altars, censers, and orisons must still be acknowledged. By implication the sun is both type and minister of Christ.

This apparently orthodox perspective becomes further evident when one contrasts these mountain-altars with Shelley's earlier description of Mont Blanc. Mont Blanc, as Shelley envisions it, is not an altar of worship but a dwelling place for "the secret Strength of things" ("Mont Blanc," l. 139). Moreover, lines 142 to 144 of "Mont Blanc" suggest that the mountain derives this symbolic significance from the transforming power of "the human mind's imaginings." The mountain-altars of "The Triumph of Life" are really the antithesis of the imaginatively perceived Mont Blanc— they are part of the paraphernalia of natural religion. Perhaps the orthodoxy of Coleridge's "Hymn before Sunrise"helped to shape this mountain imagery.[15]

If a natural perspective is maintained in lines 1 to 20, two other perspectives which may be termed "transcendent" and "orthodox" are implied with sufficient power to challenge its validity. While, as Wasserman has shown, the revelation of "Adonais" is "progressive," this opening revelation is static, the three perspectives with their diverse implications pointing in all directions at once. Thus, to return to the point initiating this discussion, the "native noon" of line 131 is rendered highly ambiguous when viewed from the vantage point of the opening lines.

But to view the "native noon" in this way, of course, is to isolate the image from the context of the imagery as a whole. Examining that total pattern from a good distance back, one discerns a swirling cone of natural images, all threatening to disengage themselves from their cycles, but all being ultimately pulled back from static center to turning circumference. This infernal maelstrom, which I analyze in the remainder of this chapter, organizes the poem's images, demonstrates its theme, is microcosmically mirrored in the whirling dance of Life's manic followers (ll. 141–54, 170–71, 453–55, 508–10), and relentlessly directs each potential analogue of eternity. Thus the sun which, as analogue of Christ and of the one Spirit, might become "the sun that never sets" or "the white radiance of Eternity," finally proceeds westward across the sky. When Shelley awakens from the vision of lines 41 to 180 to perceive Rousseau in the distorted root which grows out of the hillside, "the morn" is past (l. 193).

Similarly, Rousseau finds himself asleep (l. 311) in "the April prime" (l. 308) and awakens to "broad day" (l. 337). Some time later, although it is "broad day," sunlight flows suddenly from the east, as if it were dawn (ll. 333–34). The "shape all light" which subsequently appears is like "the Dawn / Whose invisible rain . . . seemed to sing / A silver music on the mossy lawn" (ll. 353–55). Despite this strong suggestion of a millennial dawn (cf. "Prometheus Unbound" where, at the springtime advent of the millennium, "the sun will not rise until noon" [2.5.10]), Rousseau concludes his narrative with references to autumn (ll. 528–29) and the day's decline (ll. 537–38).

The close parallel between Rousseau's narrative and Shelley's vision of lines 41 to 180 is also suggestive. The sunrise which awakens the world prompts Shelley himself to sleep (ll. 1–25), just as Rousseau finds himself asleep during "broad day" which is also dawn, in April, when the budding "forest tops" are kindled by the returning sun and "burn" like the flowers Shelley describes (ll. 9–13, 308–10). Shelley's sleep is prevented by a "strange trance" in which he perceives, first, the highway of life, and, second, the frozen light of Life's chariot. Rousseau awakens to perceive that same chariot, and his concluding vision of the men enslaved to Life strongly recalls the confused sequence of seasonal images in lines 41 to 76 of Shelley's narrative. Just as the people on Shelley's "public way" are "numerous as gnats upon the evening gleam" (l. 46), so the phantoms of Rousseau's concluding vision are "like small gnats & flies, as thick as mist / On evening marshes" (ll. 508–9). While the people Shelley sees are like "the million leaves of summer's bier" (l. 51), the "shadows" which fall away from the people in Rousseau's vision are "numerous as the dead leaves blown / In autumn evening from a poplar tree" (ll. 528–29). Both Shelley's and Rousseau's visions juxtapose images of evening (ll. 46, 529) and autumn (ll. 51, 529) with other seasonal and solar images (ll. 75–76, 511–12, 532–35) in a manner which suggests an endless natural cycle and which also suggests that Shelley and Rousseau are giving us two perspectives on the same sunrise, the same day, and the same visionary experience.[16] Against this perspective of perpetual change the analogues of eternity are set. Moreover, the complexity and speed of life's transformations seem both to increase as one nears the poem's conclusion.

For example: the phantoms of Rousseau's concluding vision are molded by the "miscreative" Car of Life (l. 533) from the *Doppelgänger* shadows of Life's captives (ll. 528–30).[17] These pestilential shades infest kings (ll. 495–96), pontiffs (ll. 496–97), and all manner of living men. The issue of this torment is a further shedding of shadowy masks (ll. 535–36) by the various victims. Life thus forces its captives to create the phantoms which cause their own decay (ll. 537–43). This process recalls the phantasmal inferno of Shelley's vision, where each traveller of life's highway walks in the gloom of his own shadow, experiencing a self-created death (ll. 58–59). Some travellers exhaust themselves by fleeing their own shadows (l. 61), while others madly pursue or "shun" the shadows thrown by the clouds (l. 63). But if, in lines 480 to 543, the Life-chariot prompts its captives to create the phantoms which destroy them, in lines 41 to 65 men seem to create their destructive shadows of their own free will. However, lines 208 to 292 reveal that Life effects its victory over man (ll. 239–40) by prompting his worship of self-created shadows. These shadows are the religious, political, and philosophical dogmas which eclipse the sun of truth (ll. 209–14, 248–51, 260–65, 288–92). Thus the infernal self-destruction of lines 480 to 543 concisely summarizes the lengthier portrayal of destructive idolatry in lines 41 to 292. The latter passage sets up at least three levels of reference for its cyclic imagery. First, there is the "true Sun" (l. 292) which is eclipsed by the shades of dogma. Then there are the shades themselves, which are presented in conjunction with seasonal images. Finally, there is the "morn of truth" feigned by the various dogmatists. Because it is not the dawn of the "true Sun," this "morn" finally gives way to evening and deep night (ll. 214–15) even as the Sun of Shelley's opening lines finally travels westward. Indeed, the impermanence of the sun and star images (ll. 78–79) makes one wonder whether Rousseau's "true Sun" and Shelley's "native noon" (l. 131) might not, like the "star" which ruled Plato (presumably the boy, Aster, l. 256) or the "noonday" of the captives (l. 64), be merely part of life's illusion.

This possibility is strengthened by the echoes of Wordsworth's Immortality Ode in Rousseau's narrative. Just as, in the ode, nature both causes "her inmate man / [to] forget" his divine origin (ll. 82–84) and, conversely, prompts thoughts of immortality (ll. 105, 189–204), so Rousseau sleeps amid a profusion of natural impressions (ll. 308–20) and, conversely, awakens to behold a "scene of woods & waters" which retains a "light diviner than the common Sun" (ll. 355–38). Rousseau then perceives a "shape all light" standing on the "floor of the fountain" (ll. 350–53, cf. Wordsworth's "fountain light of all our day"). Although this shape ultimately wanes in the "coming light" of the Life-chariot (l. 412), she still accompanies Rousseau as he moves westward (ll. 424–33), this westward movement of the invisible shape "on the stream" (l. 425) strongly recalling the similar course of the "vision" in Wordsworth's ode (ll. 72–75), as well as the westward vision of Shelley in the opening lines (ll. 26–27).[18] Just as the "birth" of Wordsworth's ode is "a . . . forgetting," so Rousseau cannot remember if, before his sleep, he had known heaven or hell (ll. 332–33). If, before Rousseau's sleep, life had been a heaven, then Nature is, as in the Immortality Ode, a nursemaid destroying her child's happy recollections. But in lines 335 to 348 the natural environment seems to reflect divinity, thus, again as in the Immortality Ode, prompting recollections of a higher reality. The positive and negative functions of Nature, which Wordsworth's ode reconciles in the last two stanzas, remain at odds in Rousseau's narrative.

Here again Rousseau's experience parallels Shelley's. Rousseau really tells us nothing of the "oblivious spell" of his sleep (l. 331) and cannot recall whether life before that sleep had been a heaven or a hell. Similarly, Shelley's nocturnal meditation involved "thoughts which must remain untold" (l. 21). The light imagery of lines 337 to 353 seems divinely beneficent but ultimately issues in the vision of the shape all light. This shape erases all thought from Rousseau's mind, even "as Day upon the threshold of the east / Treads out the lamps of night" (ll. 389–90). It is "as if the gazer's mind was strewn beneath / Her feet like embers" (ll. 385–86). Moreover, she does not erase his mind in order to make possible a new illumination; rather, she "thought by thought, / Trampled its fires into the dust of death" (ll. 387–88).

The violence of this suggests that it is finally neither the sun nor the shape all light, but rather the lamps of night (see ll. 389, 390–93) that are truly beneficent. Just as Shelley's night is, first, a mask (l. 3) stripped away by the awakener-sun, then a jewelled cone whose stars, like Rousseau, are "laid asleep" (l. 23, cf. l. 311), and, finally, by implication, a disperser of light's illusory "veil" (ll. 32–33), so Rousseau's night simile casts an ironic shadow over the apparent beneficence and permanence of the light imagery in lines 337 to 353. All this, of course, tends to dim further the promise held out by Shelley's "native noon" (l. 131).

If, in Shelley's vision, the Life-chariot eclipses the noon with its light (ll. 77–79), Rousseau sees the brilliant "shape all light" dimmed and eclipsed by that same destructive glare (l. 412 ff.). While, in her effect upon Rousseau, the shape was like the day which treads out "heaven's living eyes" (l. 492), the shape, in relation to the chariot, is like the morning star which is gradually eclipsed by sunrise (ll. 412–15). Thus, again, the illusion of permanence and power is destroyed. The shape takes unto herself both the negative implications of day and the positive implications of night. The result is confusion.

In lines 348 to 381, the shape, though brilliant enough to wear the sun's eye as corona (ll. 348–55), is veiled by Iris, the rainbow (ll. 356–57). Flinging out the dew's "invisible rain" (ll. 352–54), the shape provides both the light and the refractive medium for the rainbow. One possible implication of this process is that the white radiance of Eternity and life's dome of many-colored glass are one, or, to put it another way, the white radiance of Eternity is merely one more image on life's "false & fragile glass" (ll. 245–47). Whatever the significance of the Iris episode, this idea is certainly implicit in the solar cycle the shape follows. Although eclipsed by the light of Life's chariot, the shape nevertheless keeps her "obscure tenour" beside Rousseau's westward "path" (ll. 432–33). In lines 416 to 433 Shelley portrays the shape as an orbiting Venus which invisibly follows the westward course of Rousseau's journey and life. Thus the Venus complex which, in "The Revolt of Islam," made morning and evening star types of an eternal transcendent reality is reemployed here.[19]

But the shape's association with Venus, though first suggesting immunity from the natural flux which controls sun and seasons, ultimately proves ironic, since the shape follows both Rousseau and the sun on their westward journeys. Thus again an image threatens to disengage itself from the natural cycle, but is ultimately pulled back into that merciless flux. By suggesting, first, a sun-eclipsing light, and, second, the morning star, the shape makes two movements toward the still point of the poem's turning world, only to be twice pulled back to circumference, first by the rainbow and water imagery of lines 349 to 381, and, second, by the solar cycle followed in Rousseau's journey. Moreover, since the very advent of Life's maenadic triumph (ll. 459–68, cf. "Prometheus Unbound," 2.3.5) seems to issue from Rousseau's acceptance of the nepenthe the shape offers, her offer must, at the very least, be accounted morally ambiguous. Her accompaniment of Rousseau on his westward journey powerfully parodies the vigil of the guardian "vision" which, in Wordsworth's ode, attends the maturing man (Immortality Ode, ll. 71–76).

Since the whole episode is initiated by Rousseau's quest for enlightenment, it holds out little hope for man's pursuit of ultimate reality. The episode, like the poem as a whole, suggests that the man who, like Rousseau, seeks to learn "whence [he] came" and thus to escape life's "perpetual dream" (l. 397) will, through the very intensity of his focus upon mortal images of transcendence, become all the more deeply locked in life's sleep. The stripping away of life's veils (l. 413) is also the creation of illusion, since the anagoge of man's imaginative probings will inevitably be but one more earthly image, and reverence for this image as the hard-won transcendent reality will in fact be a reverence for life's "unwilling dross" ("Adonais," l. 384). Thus those who try hardest to escape life's cycle are those who soonest succumb ("Those soonest from whose forms most shadows past" [l. 542]). In turning the shadows its captives shed into phantoms which plague them (ll. 481–543), the Life-chariot vividly demonstrates this paradox. An obvious descendant of the chariot-visions of Ezekiel, Dante, and Milton,[20] the chariot casts an ironic light on those religious visions, just as the images of life's highway and of Rousseau's falling by the wayside (l. 541) echo Bunyan and the New Testament with similar effect.[21] Thus the orthodox perspective implicit in Shelley's opening portrayal of the rising sun is ironically developed during the course of the poem.

"The Triumph of Life" also parodies the positive visions of Shelley's earlier poetry. Perhaps the best example of this is the ironic parallel between the chariot of Life and the chariot of the Moon-spirit in act 4 of "Prometheus Unbound." I will quote the relevant passages in full:

> I see a chariot like that thinnest boat,
> In which the Mother of the Months is borne
> By ebbing light into her western cave,
> When she upsprings from interlunar dreams;
> O'er which is curved an orblike canopy
> Of gentle darkness, and the hills and woods,
> Distinctly seen through that dusk aery veil,

Regard like shapes in an enchanter's glass;
Its wheels are solid clouds . .
. . . .
                    . . they roll
And move and grow as with an inward wind;
Within it sits a winged infant, white
Its countenance, like the whiteness of bright snow,
Its plumes are as feathers of sunny frost,
Its limbs gleam white, through the wind-flowing folds
Of its white robe, woof of ethereal pearl.
Its hair is white, the brightness of white light
Scattered in strings; yet its two eyes are heavens
Of liquid darkness, which the Deity
Within seems pouring, as a storm is poured
From jagged clouds, out of their arrowy lashes,
Tempering the cold and radiant air around,
With fire that is not brightness; in its hand
It sways a quivering moonbeam, from whose point
A guiding power directs the chariot's prow.
                    ["Prometheus Unbound," 4. 206–32]

            Like the young moon

When on the sunlit limits of the night
Her white shell trembles amid crimson air
And whilst the sleeping tempest gathers might

Doth, as a herald of its coming, bear
The ghost of her dead Mother, whose dim form
Bends in dark ether from her infant's chair,

So came a chariot on the silent storm
Of its own rushing spendour, and a Shape
So sate within as one whom years deform

Beneath a dusky hood & double cape
Crouching within the shadow of a tomb,
And o'er what seemed the head, a cloud like crape,

Was bent a dun & faint etherial gloom
Tempering the light; upon the chariot's beam
A Janus-visaged Shadow did assume

The guidance of that wonder-winged team.
The Shapes which drew it in thick lightnings
Were lost: I heard alone on the air's soft stream

The music of their ever moving wings,
All the four faces of that charioteer
Had their eyes banded . . . little profit brings

Speed in the van & blindness in the rear,
Nor then avail the beams that quench the Sun
Or that his banded eyes could pierce the sphere

Of all that is, has been, or will be done—
So ill was the car guided, but it past
With solemn speed majestically on.
["Triumph of Life," ll. 78–106]

"But the new Vision, and its cold bright car,
With savage music, stunning music, crost

"The forest, and as if from some dread war
Triumphantly returning, the loud million
Fiercely extolled the fortune of her star—

"A moving arch of victory the vermilion
And green & azure plumes of Iris had
Built high over her wind-winged pavilion."
["Triumph of Life," ll. 434–41]

"Each one
Of that great crowd sent forth incessantly
These shadows . . .

. . . .
"And of this stuff the car's creative ray
Wrought all the busy phantoms that were there

"As the sun shapes the clouds."
["Triumph of Life," ll. 526–35]

The chariots of "Prometheus Unbound" and "The Triumph of
Life" are both compared to "the new moon with the old moon in its
arms." The "orblike canopy" of the Moon-spirit's chariot is "of
gentle darkness" but, despite the duskiness of its veil, reveals the
hills and woods with seemingly supernatural distinctness (ll.
211–14). In partial contrast, the Shape riding the Life-chariot
"Crouch[es] within the shadow of a tomb" (l. 90). This shadow,
with the Shape's "cloud like crape," emits a faint "gloom" which
"tempers" the light (ll. 90–93), even as the lightless fire of the
Moon-spirit's eyes "tempers" the "cold and radiant air" (l. 229).

Accompanying these parallels, however, is the ironic contrast between the Moon-spirit's tempering vision and the blindness of the Shape in the Life-chariot.

The Life-chariot's "wind-winged pavilion" has "the vermilion / And green & azure plumes of Iris" built over it as "a moving arch of victory" (ll. 439–41). This rainbow spectrum images the many-colored glass of "Adonais" and "The Triumph of Life" (ll. 245–48) as an *arc de triomphe* and thus represents, literally, the triumph of life ("Life, like a dome of many-coloured glass / Stains the white radiance of Eternity" ["Adonais," ll. 462–63]). The idea of refraction is also latent in the comparison of the Moon-chariot's "orblike canopy" to "an enchanter's glass" (l. 213). Both the Moon-spirit's chariot and the chariot of Life drastically modify perception of the environment, the former making the familiar appear strange (ll. 211–13) and the latter, ultimately, casting an apparently supernal light upon the natural environment (ll. 444–47). The extraordinarily vivid perception which the Moon-spirit's dusky veil makes possible closely parallels the vivid perception of Shelley's "strange trance" which is as the imposition of a veil over evening hills (ll. 29–33). These processes surely represent the spreading of imagination's "figured curtain" (moon-chariot, veil over hills) and its "laying bare" of the "sleeping spirit" of the paradigmatic Forms (Life-chariot's light) as described in the "Defence of Poetry."[22] But the imaginative process which, in the passage from "Prometheus Unbound," contributes to the universal light and harmony of the Promethean liberation prompts, in "The Triumph of Life," the self-destructive revelry of Life's captives (l. 444 ff.)

The Promethean "ode to joy" issues, of course, from the imaginative awakening of the fallen Prometheus, and the passage of the Moon-spirit, like the other episodes of act 4 preceding Demogorgon's concluding prophecy, portrays the process and effects of imaginative awakening. The Car of Life fulfills a similar function, but portrays the imaginative process in an exclusively negative light, prompting, first, through its brilliance, the frenzied maniacal "joy" which, in both "Prometheus Unbound" and "The Triumph of Life," characterizes the perversion of vision into idolatry (l. 444 ff., cf. "Prometheus Unbound," 2.3.5–10) and, second, the casting forth of the shadows and the molding of the phantoms (ll. 531–34), demonic portrayals of transcendent intimation ("Prometheus Unbound," 2.1.61–65) and imaginative creation respectively.[23] The Life-chariot, through the Promethean, biblical, Dantesque, and Miltonic echoes, submerges those earlier images of transcendence in the poem's infernal whirlpool.

Another metaphor the poem ironically exploits is the river of life. A cavern hides the unperceived source of Rousseau's river-world and his life is imaged as a journey beside the cavern-engendered rivers. Similarly, the source of the stream which images the "Alastor" poet's life is "inaccessibly profound" ("Alastor," ll. 502–3) and the Arve descends from the "remote and inaccessible" reaches of Mont Blanc ("Mont Blanc" ll. 16–17, 96–97, 127). These remote heights are ultimately identified as the abode of the Power or life-source. Rousseau's reiteration of the obstinate Wordsworthian questionings of the essay "On Life" ("Whence do we come?") also suggests a metaphysical significance for his journey.[24] Rousseau asks the shape all light:

> " 'If, as it doth seem,
> Thou comest from the realm without a name,
>
> " 'Into this valley of perpetual dream,
> Shew whence I came, and where I am, and why—
> Pass not away upon the passing stream.' "
>
> [Ll. 395–99]

The source of life's stream, however, remains a mystery, as the shape gives only the destructive nepenthe in reply.

Thus, to return to my original point, "The Triumph of Life" may be regarded as a poetic portrayal of metaphysical skepticism. Positing analogues of noumenal or transcendent reality, and then undermining their validity by submerging them in natural flux, the poem casts severe doubt, not only on the possibility of discovering ultimate reality, but also on the validity of the transcendence concept itself. For it ultimately makes no difference whether the "native noon" is the Platonic Heaven, Kant's noumenal reality, the "Power," or the clockmaker God of the Deists; the analogue is undermined by its context, as indeed are all the analogues of eternity or "ultimate reality" which the poem presents. Once this process has been completed we are left adrift amid Humean uncertainty. Can man achieve certain knowledge of anything? Through its self-destructive imagery, "The Triumph of Life" focuses this philosophical problem with an intensity and power surely unsurpassed in English Romanticism. It also ends Shelley's mature career where it began: in the unresolved enigmas of "Alastor."

CONCLUSION

IN the poems I have examined skepticism is the motive force. Shelley's particularized metaphysical distinctions and particularized images feed and refine each other to a point where each poem redefines its predecessor. This process reflects Shelley's constant reassessment and revision of his own ideas. A catholic and voracious scholar, Shelley was open-minded to a degree that would surely frighten most individuals. All philosophical positions that seemed plausible to him were experienced personally through poetic transmutation. Shelley's self-qualifying and self-negating poetic method demonstrates the value, as well as the dangers, of a skeptical attitude to life. I will briefly summarize how it does so.

Certain key terms recur frequently in Shelley's poetry and prose from "Alastor" to "Prometheus Unbound." Of these the two most important are *power* and *vacancy*. *Vacancy*, as defined in the essay "On Life" (1819), is ignorance of life's source. In seeking to know "the thrilling secrets of the birth of time," the poet of "Alastor" pursues life's source at the expense of normal social attachments. Because of his lack of involvement with the human community, the socially valuable insights which might have resulted from his skeptical pursuit of truth are forgotten in the quest for a phantom born of his own mind.

The "Hymn to Intellectual Beauty" and "Mont Blanc" redefine the occult "secrets" of "Alastor" as the inscrutable "power" underlying phenomena. Both poems demonstrate the necessary relationship between intuition of that power and social iconoclasm. While "Alastor" proceeds largely through obscure allegory and ambiguous natural description, "Mont Blanc" and the Hymn present their metaphysical skepticism in an organized, cogent manner. The natural description of "Mont Blanc" is at once very extensive and very particularized and, unlike the natural description of "Alastor," it corresponds at every point with the skeptical view of reality it symbolizes.

This consistency in "Mont Blanc" springs from the concept of a collective consciousness. The concept heightens Shelley's sense of social interdependence and precludes the pessimistic view that the objects of perception die with their perceiver. The universe of "Mont Blanc" and the Hymn is "everlasting" because it is everlastingly perceived by the successive generations of mankind. In "Alastor," where the idea of a collective consciousness is absent, there is no such sense of permanence or community.

However, the "secret springs" of human perception in "Mont Blanc" have their origin in the "inaccessible" source of the "Alastor" life-stream ("Alastor," ll. 502-14). Moreover, both "Mont Blanc" and the Hymn acknowledge that imaginative intimation of the "power" may prove privately and publicly destructive, should the individual define the object of his intimation in dogmatic terms. The poet of "Alastor" did this when he worshipped the veiled maiden.

"The Revolt of Islam" presents the skepticism of "Alastor," "Mont Blanc," and the Hymn in a quasi-epic framework. "The Revolt" avoids the determinism of "Queen Mab" by locating the power outside of time, thus making historical progress dependent upon human skepticism, rather than upon the clash of superhuman forces. Cythna's messianic activity and, ultimately, her transcendence are rooted in a descent into the cave of her own mind.

Similarly, Asia's transcendent union with Prometheus follows upon the confirmation of her own skepticism in the mind-cave of Demogorgon. However, once Asia and Prometheus are reunited, they do not, like Laon and Cythna, ascend to a transcendent temple, but, instead, enter a paradisal cave whence they commune, from a distance, with humanity. While their union brings about the millennium, their separation from men reflects Shelley's increasing skepticism about man's capacity totally to eliminate tyranny. This skepticism is even more intensely manifested in the separation of the Witch of Atlas from the enslaved human community with which she intermittently communes, and it reaches its apogee in the portrayal of Urania (symbol of divine inspiration) as time-bound and passive. This negative portrayal of the muse of Keats and Milton calls the social value of imaginative vision into serious question.

The poems discuss skepticism at the same time as they demonstrate it. Initially, under the influence of Hume and Drummond, Shelley embraces skepticism as a powerful weapon against social injustice. But, since Shelley's skepticism is contingent upon imaginative vision and since, as "Prometheus Unbound," "The Witch of Atlas," and "Adonais" all show, man's capacity for imaginative vision is severely limited, Shelley's skepticism is ultimately concerned more with this limitation than with the defeat of socially destructive dogma.

Shelley's most ingenious way of focusing this concern is by shifting his main attention from those protagonists who are embroiled in earthly struggle (the wandering poet in "Alastor," the author himself in "Mont Blanc" and the Hymn, Laon and Cythna in "The Revolt of Islam," Prometheus in the first act of "Prometheus Unbound") to those protagonists who stand above the battle and can thus delineate man's limitations (the united Asia and Prometheus in act 3 of "Prometheus Unbound," Demogorgon in act 4 of "Prometheus Unbound," the Witch in "The Witch of Atlas," Urania, and in the last stanzas, Keats, Shelley, and all "the immortals" in "Adonais"). Thus, while similar "plots" and image-patterns recur from poem to poem, the perspective from which they are viewed continually shifts. While "The Revolt of

Islam" is a narrative mirror of the expository "Mont Blanc," "Prometheus Unbound," "The Witch of Atlas," and "Adonais" are increasingly more parodic mirrors of "The Revolt of Islam." Since each of Shelley's poems is an objectification of his own mind at the time of writing, this constant redefinition reflects his own skeptical qualification of each intellectual position he embraces.

The kaleidoscopic shifting of thematic implication in "Adonais" and "The Triumph of Life" is masterfully handled. Indeed, few poets are as adept as Shelley at the particularized redefinition of symbols. Shelley's skepticism fostered the development of this technique to the level of consummate mastery which "Adonais" and "The Triumph of Life" both display. And without this techni- cal mastery Shelley's expression of skepticism would lose its great cogency and power. Thus the theme of skepticism and the device for its expression strengthen and refine one another. Skepticism, more than any other factor, is responsible for the steadily increasing artistic excellence of Shelley's work from 1815 to the end. This mastery accelerates remarkably at the close of Shelley's life, precisely at the time when his skepticism was most intense.

However, "The Triumph of Life" is much more than the consummation of Shelley's technical development. It represents also a new beginning in his expression of skepticism. This becomes especially clear when its relationship to "Alastor," "Mont Blanc," and "Prometheus Unbound" is considered. In concluding this study I will briefly explore the nature of this new beginning.

Throughout my study I have distinguished between Shelley's "empirical" and "Platonic" skepticism. The former, encouraging doubt of all dogma, undermines public tyranny. The latter, which doubts imaginative vision, undermines private faith. But the impossibility of private faith can be either welcomed or regretted in Shelley's poetry. "Prometheus Unbound" does both, especially in act 3. Act 3 moves between a pastoral and an urbane perspective; between an unambitious delight in what is knowable (e.g., 3.4.73–76) and a restless fascination with what is not ("the intense inane," 3.4.204).

This ambivalence seems, at first, to have no more than personal significance. But this is a false impression. When closely studied, the act makes clear that public salvation depends upon the private acceptance of the limitations of the human mind.

Perhaps the temple best focuses this connection. To the private mind, the distant temple by the crystalline pool is attractive (3.3.159–61); it conjures images of transcendence (ll. 170–75). But that temple is also the product of public hysteria (ll. 124–30), and the "faithless" enthusiasm it induces (l. 130) is not "faithless" because it is skeptical, but because it is intellectually irresponsible (l. 129); because fanaticism breaks faith with the mind.

Indeed, with its many implications, the term "faithless faith" (l. 130) could well be the logos of Shelley's poetic universe. The "mild" faith of "Mont Blanc" (l. 77), for example, is faithless because it distrusts all dogma, but faithful and mild in accepting the mind's limitations. If "The Witch of Atlas," "Adonais," and "The Triumph of Life" reveal an increasing dissatisfaction with those limitations, they also demonstrate with greater and greater clarity the need to accept them. The universe of "The Triumph of Life" is an inferno because the value of everything in it depends upon its accuracy as an analogue of something beyond human knowledge. Such a criterion of value is not only absurd, it is itself as destructive as any of the various "faiths" the poem condemns.

But the criterion is not without value either. It prompts a systematic demonstration of the mind's inability to transcend its limitations. Although "The Triumph of Life" reexpresses the total skepticism of "Alastor," it does so with a thoroughness and authority far beyond the reach of the earlier poem. The tension which informs "The Triumph of Life" is not, as in "Alastor," a confused ambivalence; it is a sustained battle between the limits of Shelley's knowledge and the limits of his desire. In the terms of the third act of "Prometheus Unbound," this contest opposes "empirical" to "Platonic" skepticism: it sets a public insistence on the mind's limits against a private desire to transcend them.

There can be little doubt what would have emerged from this contest, had the poet lived past 1822. In "The Triumph of Life," Shelley is like Prometheus in the first act of "Prometheus Unbound." Although Prometheus verbally commits himself to forgiveness, he must suffer through many infernal visions before that outward commitment deepens to inner conviction. Likewise, Shelley declares the mind's limits by 1815, and in the third act of "Prometheus Unbound" shows both the advantages of accepting those limits and the dangers of denying them. But Shelley, too, must suffer through many infernal visions; must test the limits repeatedly before uniting public and private, "empirical" and "Platonic," skepticism. "The Triumph of Life" represents this testing: it is a second and greater "Alastor," an inferno which, like "The Fall of Hyperion," humanizes mythical suffering and invalidates the pursuit of a private transcendence. It conclusively shows the futility of such a pursuit by repudiating all analogues and concepts of transcendence, thus destroying all basis for faith in a transcendent realm. After this work, it is highly unlikely that there could have been any further separation between Shelley's private and public skepticism. Now there could be no private quest for eternity. There would have been no gods in the new millennium.

NOTES

PREFACE

1. C. E. Pulos, *The Deep Truth: A Study of Shelley's Scepticism* (Lincoln: University of Nebraska Press, 1954; Bison Books, 1962).

2. Earl R. Wasserman, *Shelley: A Critical Reading* (Baltimore: Johns Hopkins University Press, 1971), pp. 484–85.

3. Donald H. Reiman, *Shelley's "The Triumph of Life": A Critical Study* (Urbana: University of Illinois Press, 1965), p. ix.

4. Richard Harter Fogle, *The Imagery of Keats and Shelley* (Chapel Hill: University of North Carolina Press, 1949).

5. Reiman, *Shelley's "The Triumph of Life,"* pp. 11–18, 22–23.

6. Wasserman, *Shelley*, pp. 11–41.

INTRODUCTION

1. C. E. Pulos, *The Deep Truth: A Study of Shelley's Scepticism* (Lincoln: University of Nebraska Press, 1954; Bison Books, 1962); Hoxie Neale Fairchild, *The Romantic Quest* (New York: Columbia University Press, 1931); Floyd Stovall, "Shelley's Doctrine of Love," *PMLA* 45 (1930): 283–303; Benjamin Kurtz, *The Pursuit of Death: A Study of Shelley's Poetry* (New York: Oxford University Press, 1933); D. J. Kapstein, "The Meaning of Shelley's 'Mont Blanc,'" *PMLA* 62 (1947): 1046–60.

2. Earl R. Wasserman, *Shelley: A Critical Reading* (Baltimore: Johns Hopkins University Press, 1971), pp. 222–38.

3. "Mont Blanc," 11. 80–83. All quotations from the poetry in this chapter are from *Shelley: Poetical Works*, ed. Thomas Hutchinson, rev. G. M. Matthews, 2d ed. (London: Oxford University Press, 1970).

4. William Drummond, *Academical Questions* (London, 1805), I, 5. For several striking parallels between Shelley's arguments and phrasing (both in prose and poetry) and those of Drummond, see F. L. Jones, "Shelley's 'On Life,'" *PMLA* 62 (1947): 774–83.

5. David Hume, *A Treatise of Human Nature* and *Dialogues Concerning Natural Religion* in *Philosophical Works*, ed. T. H. Green and T. H. Grosse, 4 vols. (London, 1896, reprint ed. Aalen: Scientia Publishers, 1964), 1:499–500, 2:398 ff.

6. Percy Bysshe Shelley in D. L. Clark, ed., *Shelley's Prose or The Trumpet of a Prophecy* (Albuquerque: University of New Mexico Press, 1954), pp. 196–214; also *Shelley and his Circle*, vol. 5, ed. Donald H. Reiman (Cambridge, Mass.: Harvard University Press, 1973), 5:246.

7. Influential explications of "Alastor" and "The Revolt of Islam" are discussed in chapters 1 and 2.

8. Ross Woodman, *The Apocalyptic Vision in the Poetry of Shelley* (Toronto: University of Toronto Press, 1964), p. 3.

9. Notably Milton Wilson, *Shelley's Later Poetry* (New York: Columbia University Press, 1959), pp. 298–99. See also Wilson's perceptive reconsideration of this question in his review of Earl R. Wasserman's *Shelley: A Critical Reading* in *English Language Notes*, 11 (1973): 64–68. Ross Woodman's review of the same book also posits a convincing resolution of this question; *Keats-Shelley Journal* 21–22 (1972–73): 244–52.

10. "On Life," in *Shelley's Prose*, ed. Clark, p. 173; also *Shelley's Poetry and Prose*, ed. Donald H. Reiman and Sharon B. Powers (New York: W. W. Norton, 1977), p. 476.

11. See Pulos, *The Deep Truth*, pp. 67–68.

12. Harold Bloom, *Shelley's Mythmaking* (Ithaca: Cornell University Press, 1969), p. vii.

CHAPTER ONE

1. Raymond D. Havens, "Shelley's 'Alastor'" *PMLA* 45 (1930): 1098–1115.

2. Ibid., p. 1109.

3. "Evil genius" was Thomas Love Peacock's translation of the term *alastor*. Peacock proposed the title.

4. Hughes, Du Bois, and Wier insist that the "evil genius" of the title and the "furies" of the preface are active in the poem itself, but their description and definitions of these entities differ radically. See A. M. D. Hughes, "Alastor, or The Spirit of Solitude," *Modern Language Review* 43 (1948): 465–70; Arthur E. Du Bois, "Alastor: The Spirit of Solitude,"

Journal of English and Germanic Philology 35 (1936): 530–45; Marion Clyde Wier, "Shelley's 'Alastor' Again," *PMLA* 46 (1931): 947–50. For Gibson, the dream-maiden represents merely a vision of a perfect companion, for Du Bois a transcendent herald of the millennium, for Jones "a symbol of all truth and beauty," for Baker a dramatization of the nympholepsy to which Shelley was prone, and for Hoffman a narcissistic self-projection. See E. K. Gibson, "'Alastor': A Reinterpretation," *PMLA* 62 (1947): 1029; F. L. Jones, "The Vision Theme in Shelley's 'Alastor' and Related Works," *Studies in Philology* 44 (1947): 109; Carlos Baker, *Shelley's Major Poetry: The Fabric of a Vision* (Princeton: Princeton University Press, 1948), pp. 41–60; H. L. Hoffman, *An Odyssey of the Soul: Shelley's "Alastor"* (New York: Columbia University Press, 1933), p. 34. Attempts to detect allegory have ranged from the biographical (Hughes says the veiled maid is Mary), to a general insistence on the parallels between the hero's psychological conflicts and Shelley's, to attempts to prove that Wordsworth or Coleridge is the prototype of the hero. See Paul Mueschke and E. L. Griggs, "Wordsworth as the Prototype of the Poet in Shelley's 'Alastor,'" *PMLA* 49 (1934): 229–45; M. Kessel, "The Poet in Shelley's 'Alastor': A Criticism," *PMLA* 51 (1936): 302–10; Joseph Raben, "Coleridge as the Prototype of the Poet in Shelley's 'Alastor,'" *Review of English Studies* 17 (1966): 142–56.

5. Milton Wilson, *Shelley's Later Poetry* (New York: Columbia University Press, 1959), p. 164.

6. For *love* see David Perkins, ed., *English Romantic Writers* (New York, Chicago: Harcourt, Brace and World, 1967), p. 959; for *imagination* see Harold Bloom, *The Visionary Company*, rev. ed. (Ithaca: Cornell University Press, 1971), p. 285.

7. "Queen Mab," 6.233–38 in *Shelley: Poetical Works*, ed. Thomas Hutchinson, rev. G. M. Matthews, 2d ed. (London: Oxford University Press, 1970). Quotations from the poetry in this chapter depart from the Oxford text only in the third stanza of the Hymn, where I incorporate Judith Chernaik's correction. See Judith Chernaik, "Textual Emendations for Three Poems," *Keats-Shelley Journal* 19 (1970): 44–48; also Judith Chernaik, *The Lyrics of Shelley* (Cleveland and London: Case Western Reserve University Press, 1972), p. 186.

8. F. S. Ellis, *A Lexical Concordance to the Poetical Works of Shelley* (London: Quaritch, 1892), p. 752. Ellis concerns himself with "Laon and Cythna," the earliest published version of "The Revolt of Islam," but its differences from its revision do not affect my claims about *power* and *vacancy*. Although largely irrelevant to my own concern, the bibliographical and historical details of the subject are well presented by Reiman. In referring to poetry preceding "Alastor," I include the Esdaile Notebook and the other early verse in *Shelley and his Circle*. It is notewor-

thy that, in this early work, the term *power* frequently employed, almost invariably denotes tyranny. See *Shelley and his Circle* vol. 5, ed. Donald H. Reiman (Cambridge, Mass.: Harvard University Press, 1973), 5:141–89; *Shelley and his Circle*, vols. 1–4, ed. K. N. Cameron, (Cambridge, Mass.: Harvard University Press, 1961, 1970), vols. 2, 4.

9. See F. L. Jones, "Shelley's 'On Life,'" *PMLA* 62 (1947): 774–83, and Donald Reiman, ed., *Shelley and his Circle*, 6:956, 971. Although Reiman proves that Jones's dating of "On Life" as roughly contemporary with "Alastor" is incorrect, Jones has nevertheless provided conclusive evidence that "On Life" represents Shelley's response to Wordsworth and Drummond, influences with which the poet grappled at all stages of his mature career. In the years 1815 to 1816 Shelley read deeply in both authors. The thematic relevance of "On Life" to "Alastor," "Mont Blanc," and the Hymn makes it essential that it be studied *with* them, regardless of chronology. The late date of the essay (1819) illustrates the chronological consistency of Shelley's skepticism.

10. "On Life" in D. L. Clark, ed., *Shelley's Prose or The Trumpet of a Prophecy* (Albuquerque: University of New Mexico Press, 1954), p. 173.

11. "The Science of Metaphysics," in ibid., p. 182.

12. Cf. *Complete Poetic Works of Shelley*, ed. Neville Rogers, 2 vols. to date (Clarendon Press: Oxford, 1975–), 2:352. Rogers's editing of Shelley's poems has cast disappointingly little light on their thematic development. Accordingly, I have chosen to retain the Hutchinson edition as my basic text, except in the case of "The Triumph of Life," a poem much clarified by Reiman's editing. The excellent new Norton edition, important for reference, is impractical as a working text because it omits so much essential material. But Rogers's editing seems perverse by comparison with Reiman's. It may well be true, as Rogers claims, that the *but* of line 79 of "Mont Blanc" results from Shelley's miscopying of his own draft, but the substitution of *in* for *but* does not significantly alter the meaning, since the "faith" to which Shelley refers is still faith in a realm beyond nature and, whether one is reconciled with nature by such faith (Hymn) or alienated from it ("Alastor"), the faith still results from the transcendental intimations nature makes possible. If Rogers were fully aware of the meaning of "Mont Blanc" he could hardly assert that *but* is "nonsensical." Although Reiman and Powers retain *but*, they are wrong when they suggest that it means "only." Its only possible meaning is "except": "except for such faith" is clear English, while "only for such faith" is not English at all; it is obscurity. See *Shelley's Poetry and Prose*, ed. Donald H. Reiman and Sharon B. Powers (New York: W. W. Norton, 1977), p. 91.

13. "Defence of Poetry," in Clark, ed., *Shelley's Prose*, p. 294.

14. Ibid., p. 295.

15. See Glenn O'Malley's excellent study, "'Alastor' and the Air Prism" in his *Shelley and Synesthesia* (Evanston: Northwestern University Press, 1964).

16. Wasserman argues that, because Shelley wrote fictional prose introductions to "Julian and Maddalo" and "Epipsychidion," he does not address us directly in the preface to "Alastor." This is an illogical argument. See Earl R. Wasserman, *Shelley: A Critical Reading* (Baltimore: Johns Hopkins University Press, 1971), p. 39.

17. Ibid., p. 15.

18. "On Life," in Clark, ed., *Shelley's Prose*, p. 172.

19. See Wasserman's discussion, in *Shelley*, pp. 11–46. The discussion of "Mont Blanc" (pp. 222–38) is the single most perceptive exegesis I have ever read.

20. Gibson says that the thrilling secrets are the wisdom of the ancients. The poet is in Ethiopia, Volney's "cradle of the sciences," an appropriate place to find the secret of life. See Gibson, "'Alastor': A Reinterpretation," p. 1027; Reiman and Powers, eds., *Shelley's Poetry and Prose*, p. 73.

21. "On Life,," in Clark, ed., *Shelley's Prose*, p. 173; also Reiman, ed., *Shelley and his Circle*, 6:971.

22. K. N. Cameron, "'Rasselas' and 'Alastor': A Study in Transmutation," *Studies in Philology*, 40 (1943): 58–78.

23. See Gibson, "'Alastor': A Reinterpretation," pp. 1042–43.

24. For a virtually definitive analysis of these difficulties in "Queen Mab" see Ross Woodman, *The Apocalyptic Vision in the Poetry of Shelley* (Toronto: University of Toronto Press, 1964), pp. 75–87.

CHAPTER TWO

1. "Prometheus Unbound," 2.4.114–20 in *Shelley: Poetical Works*, ed. Thomas Hutchinson, rev. G. M. Matthews, 2d ed. (London: Oxford University Press, 1970); quotations from the poetry throughout this chapter are from this edition.

2. Notably by Harold Bloom in *The Visionary Company*, rev. ed. (Ithaca: Cornell University Press, 1971), p. 283.

3. "On Life" in D. L. Clark, ed., *Shelley's Prose or The Trumpet of a Prophecy* (Albuquerque: University of New Mexico Press, 1954), p. 173.

4. "On Metaphysics," in ibid., p. 182.

5. "On Life," in ibid., p. 175.

6. "The Revolt of Islam," 7.31.3100–03. E. B. Murray claims that "with relatively unimportant exceptions, all of Shelley's longer poems" are in the new Norton edition. But "The Revolt of Islam" is almost completely excluded and, far from being unimportant, it is essential to an adequate appreciation of Shelley's work. Indeed, "The Revolt of Islam"

is more centrally significant than other long works which were included in full, notably "Hellas" and "Peter Bell the Third." Clearly the vital importance of "The Revolt of Islam" in the Shelley canon is still not understood. See E. B. Murray's review, *Keats-Shelley Journal* 27 (1978): 167–68, and *Shelley's Poetry and Prose*, ed. Donald H. Reiman and Sharon B. Powers (New York: W. W. Norton, 1977), pp. 96–101.

7. "Difficulty of Analyzing the Human Mind," in Clark, ed., *Shelley's Prose*, pp. 185–86.

8. See "To Mary," verse preface to "The Witch of Atlas."

9. My investigation of the star imagery was initiated by Glenn O'Malley's remarkably perceptive study in his *Shelley and Synesthesia* (Evanston: Northwestern University Press, 1964), pp. 61–70.

10. The subject of Pythagorean harmony is complex and controversial. I am merely suggesting a general (and vague) association here, which recurs in other parts of the poem, most notably in 7.32.3109–17.

11. This explains Baker's observation that Laon seems to seek martyrdom. Carlos Baker, *Shelley's Major Poetry: The Fabric of a Vision* (Princeton: Princeton University Press, 1948), p. 81.

12. See James A. Notopoulos, *The Platonism of Shelley: A Study of Platonism and the Poetic Mind* (Durham: Duke University Press, 1949), p. 440; also Reiman and Powers, eds., *Shelley's Poetry and Prose*, p. 212.

13. Edmund Spenser's Archimago is recalled both in stanza 18 of "The Witch of Atlas" and in 4.4 ff. of "The Revolt of Islam." See Carlos Baker and D. L. Clark, "Literary Sources of Shelley's 'The Witch of Atlas,'" *PMLA* 56 (1941): 472–94. The woman of canto one is probably Cynthna, despite discrepancies; e.g., the Paris episode has no parallel in canto two. Canto one is a preliminary allegory, encouraging Shelley's contemporaries to see in what follows the universal features of the French Revolution.

14. "Difficulty of Analyzing the Human Mind," in Clark, ed., *Shelley's Prose*, p. 186.

15. Letter to Godwin, 11 December 1817, in F. L. Jones, ed., *Letters of Percy Bysshe Shelley*, 2 vols. (Oxford: Clarendon Press, 1964), 1:577.

16. Preface to "The Revolt of Islam," in *Shelley: Poetical Works*, ed. Hutchinson, p. 37.

17. See S. F. Gingerich, "Shelley's Doctrine of Necessity versus Christianity," *PMLA* 33 (1918): 461–62; Earl R. Wasserman, *Shelley: A Critical Reading* (Baltimore: Johns Hopkins University Press, 1971), p. 106; Wasserman, *Shelley's "Prometheus Unbound": A Critical Reading* (Baltimore: Johns Hopkins University Press, 1965), pp. 149–50; Adel Salama, *Shelley's Major Poems: A Reinterpretation* (Salzburg: Institute of English Studies, University of Salzburg, 1973), p. 76. For Gingerich, Laon, Cythna, and their persecutors are mere pawns in a Manichaean duel

between the spirits of good and evil. Wasserman, who does not give the poem the close scrutiny it deserves, supports Gingerich, claiming that "The Revolt" posits "an ultimate cause of evil outside the human mind." Bloom also speaks disparagingly of the poem's "dualism" in *Shelley's Mythmaking* (Ithaca: Cornell University Press, 1969), p. 8. None of these positions are compatible with Cythna's assertions that the human mind can totally eliminate evil. The cursory, dismissive manner in which these authors treat the poem is fairly representative of how its importance has been underestimated.

18. "Defence of Poetry," in Clark, ed., *Shelley's Prose*, p. 293.

19. See Woodman, *The Apocalyptic Vision in the Poetry of Shelley* (Toronto: University of Toronto Press, 1964) pp. 88–102. He treats the poem as a sort of "dry run" for "Prometheus Unbound" while Baker (*Shelley's Major Poetry*, pp. 61–86) concentrates on sources and influences.

20. Ellsworth Barnard, *Shelley's Religion* (Minneapolis: University of Minnesota Press, 1937), pp. 236–38; Seymour Reiter, *A Study of Shelley's Poetry* (Albuquerque: University of New Mexico Press, 1967), pp. 35–38; Archibald Strong, *Three Studies in Shelley* (London: Oxford University Press, 1921), especially p. 25.

21. Letter to Godwin, 11 December 1817, in Jones, ed., *Letters of Shelley*, 1:577.

CHAPTER THREE

1. See Milton Wilson, *Shelley's Later Poetry* (New York: Columbia University Press, 1959), p. 64; also Earl R. Wasserman, *Shelley's "Prometheus Unbound": A Critical Reading* (Baltimore: Johns Hopkins University Press, 1965) pp. 37–38. For one other source of the "double" idea see Ross Woodman, *The Apocalyptic Vision in the Poetry of Shelley* (Toronto: University of Toronto Press, 1964), pp. 107–16.

2. I do not agree with Milton Wilson that "the moment of conversion occurs in line 53" (see Wilson, *Shelley's Later Poetry*, p. 56); I suggest rather that the conversion is in process throughout the act, as we witness a gradual deepening from verbal commitment to inner conviction.

3. "Defence of Poetry" in D. L. Clark, ed., *Shelley's Prose or The Trumpet of a Prophecy* (Albuquerque: University of New Mexico Press, 1954), p. 295.

4. "Prometheus Unbound," 3.1.37–42 in *Shelley: Poetical Works*, ed. Thomas Hutchinson, rev. G. M. Matthews, 2d ed. (London: Oxford University Press, 1970), the main source for quotations from the poetry in this chapter.

5. See Wasserman, *Shelley's "Prometheus Unbound,"* p. 91.

6. This idea is central to Wasserman's argument in *Shelley's "Prometheus Unbound."*

7. Wilson, *Shelley's Later Poetry*, pp. 63–64. One may, however, distinguish the two as varieties of man-created evil. While Milton Wilson points out similarities between the fallen Prometheus and Jupiter, Earl Wasserman and Ross Woodman both go farther than this, in effect *identifying* the unregenerate Prometheus with Jupiter and the phantasm of Jupiter. See Earl R. Wasserman, *Shelley: A Critical Reading* (Baltimore: Johns Hopkins University Press, 1971), pp. 257–61, and Woodman, *The Apocalyptic Vision*, pp. 107–8, 110–11, 115–16, 136–37, 148. I am indebted here to both arguments.

8. From *Shelley's "Prometheus Unbound": The Text and the Drafts*, ed. L. J. Zillman (New Haven: Yale University Press, 1968), p. 187. In my opinion the recent emendations and corrections made by Shelley's textual critics have not significantly altered the content of his poetry. Here colons after *man* in lines 194 and 197 emphasize the qualifying function of the twice-used *but* and clear up some syntactical obscurity. The reference to man's limitations (i.e., "just, gentle, wise—but [still, after all, only] man") is underscored by this punctuation.

9. I do not mean to suggest that this "metaphysical" perspective on Shelley's language is the only valid perspective. If that were so the act would be remarkably undramatic. In the next chapter I reexamine the passage in a more conventional light.

10. "Defence of Poetry," in Clark, ed., *Shelley's Prose*, p. 285.

CHAPTER FOUR

1. Shelley's assertions of his theme's inexpressibility have provoked violent responses from the New Critics. *Dizzy* and *lost* are undoubtedly among the words which Davie would dismiss as "reach-me-down jargon." See Donald Davie, *Purity of Diction in English Verse* (London: Chatto & Windus, 1952), p. 151. The "dying fall" exemplifies for Tate how Shelley's "mechanical" poetic method fails either to comprehend or express human experience. See Allen Tate, *Reactionary Essays on Poetry and Ideas* (New York: Charles Scribner's Sons, 1936), pp. 84–85, 93–98. The lyric as a whole employs much of the "fondled vocabulary" Leavis deplored: veils, brightness, faintness, etc. See F. R. Leavis, *Revaluation: Tradition and Development in English Poetry* (1936; reprint ed., New York: W. W. Norton, 1963), p. 215 ff. All these criticisms are marred by misreadings of Shelley.

2. See A. B. Ballman, "The Dating of Shelley's Prose Fragments, 'On Life,' 'On Love,' 'On the Punishment of Death,'" *ELH* 11 (1935):332–35. Ballman dates "On Love" at 1819 or 1820 because "the notion of an emotional nucleus is not met with in any of Shelley's earlier works but figures prominently in 'The Coliseum' and 'Epipsychidion.'" To this evidence Notopoulos adds the discernible influence of *The Symposium*,

translated by Shelley in 1818. See James A. Notopoulos, "The Dating of Shelley's Prose," *PMLA* 58 (1943): 447–98. Reiman provides conclusive evidence for 1818 in *Shelley and his Circle*, Vol. 6, ed. Donald H. Reiman (Cambridge: Harvard University Press, 1973), 6:638 ff. The fragment, however, as Clark has noted, is clearly relevant to "Alastor," and it expresses a tendency of Shelley's nature which was present from earliest youth. See D. L. Clark, "The Dates and Sources of Shelley's Metaphysical, Moral, and Religious Essays," *University of Texas Studies in English* 27 (1949): 160–94, and K. N. Cameron, *The Young Shelley: Genesis of a Radical* (New York: Macmillan, 1950), p. 30.

3. "On Love" in D. L. Clark, ed., *Shelley's Prose or The Trumpet of a Prophecy* (Albuquerque: University of New Mexico Press, 1954), p. 170.

4. "A Discourse on the Manners of the Ancient Greeks Relative to the Subject of Love," in ibid., p. 220.

5. See James A. Notopoulos, *The Platonism of Shelley: A Study of Platonism and the Poetic Mind* (Durham: Duke University Press, 1949), opening chapters; also C. E. Pulos, *The Deep Truth: A Study of Shelley's Scepticism* (Lincoln: University of Nebraska Press, 1954; Bison Books, 1962), pp. 67–88. Both men point out significant differences between Platonism proper and the more skeptical and intuitive position of Shelley.

6. From Shelley's translation of *The Symposium* in *Complete Works of Percy Bysshe Shelley*, ed. Roger Ingpen and Walter E. Peck, 10 vols. (New York: Gordian Press, 1965), 7:206.

7. "Prometheus Unbound," 2.1.62–65 in *Shelley: Poetical Works*, ed. Thomas Hutchinson, rev. G. M. Matthews, 2d ed. (London: Oxford University Press, 1970); quotations from the poetry throughout this chapter are from this edition.

8. I emphasize that, in using this terminology, I refer merely to Shelley's utilization of Platonic concepts as metaphors for noumenal reality. The role of the Orphic tradition in molding Shelley's myth is cogently discussed in Ross Woodman's *The Apocalyptic Vision in the Poetry of Shelley* (Toronto: University of Toronto Press, 1964), especially part 1.

9. See ibid., pp. 25–39.

10. I would emphasize the infantile, regressive quality in the act 3 restoration of the Saturnian age, while Woodman (ibid., pp. 138–50) tends to see it primarily as a manifestation of imaginative mastery over nature.

11. See Earl R. Wasserman, *Shelley's "Prometheus Unbound": A Critical Reading* (Baltimore: Johns Hopkins University Press, 1965). Wasserman sees Prometheus as the One Mind: the totality of intelligence of which the individual mind is but a part. I see Prometheus rather as a hypothetical individual mind of superhuman perceptual capacity. For a very

positive perspective on the Prometheus of act 3 see Bennett Weaver, *Prometheus Unbound* (Ann Arbor: University of Michigan Press, 1957).

12. Samuel Taylor Coleridge, *Biographia Literaria*, chap. 13.

13. In this connection, one may note the possible derivation of the list of human accomplishments in act 4 (l. 406 ff.) from the famous "ode to man" in Sophocles' *Antigone*, vv. 332–72.

14. "And I heard a great voice out of heaven saying, 'Behold, the tabernacle of God is with men, and he will dwell with them, and they shall be his people, and God himself shall be with them, and be their God'" (Revelation [AV] 21:3).

15. "The controlling reference . . . is to the lampadephoria, the torch race in which youths ran from the altar of Prometheus in the Academy to the Acropolis in Athens, the victory going to the first to arrive with his torch unextinguished." Shelley's source was Pausanias, *The Description of Greece*, trans. Thomas Taylor, 3 vols. (London, 1824; 1st ed., 1817), 3:224–25. See Wasserman, *Shelley's "Prometheus Unbound,"* p. 74; also E. P. Hungerford, *Shores of Darkness* (New York: Columbia University Press, 1941), pp. 197–98.

16. Letter to Godwin, 11 December 1817, in F. L. Jones, *Letters of Percy Bysshe Shelley*, 2 vols. (Oxford: Clarendon Press, 1964), 1:577.

17. 1 Cor. (AV) 15:51.

18. I postpone consideration of the Moon-spirit's chariot to my chapter on "The Triumph of Life"

19. See Harold Bloom, *Shelley's Mythmaking* (Ithaca: Cornell University Press, 1969), pp. 139–42.

20. "For man . . . sees all things thro' the narrow chinks of his cavern" (William Blake, "The Marriage of Heaven and Hell").

21. See Northrop Frye, *Anatomy of Criticism* (Princeton: Princeton University Press, 1957), pp. 182–85; also Frye's *A Natural Perspective: The Development of Shakespearean Comedy and Romance* (New York: Columbia University Press, 1965), p. 123.

22. See Carl Grabo, *The Meaning of "The Witch of Atlas"* (Chapel Hill: University of North Carolina Press, 1935), pp. 99–100. He regards stanzas 70 to 71 as evidence of the Witch's ability to nurse the soul through its transition from earthly existence to life in a Neoplatonic Heaven. But I suggest that, like Thel or the figures on the Grecian Urn, this figure will be forever *about to* change. This is why its cradle is also a casket.

23. Wasserman shows that Shelley knew the Orphic significance of this fire-water symbolism, mainly from his reading of Proclus and Porphyry in the translations of Thomas Taylor. See Earl R. Wasserman, *Shelley: A Critical Reading* (Baltimore: Johns Hopkins University Press, 1971), pp. 466–67. Note the emphasis on the symbolism in stanzas 2, 13 to 25, 28 to 30, 32 to 33, 35 to 37.

24. The arts involved in this passage (4.270–318) do not parallel exactly those described in act 2 (2.4.64–99), but the passage nevertheless provides a structural parallel with Asia's earlier description of Prometheus's gifts to man. In Shelley's "Prometheus Unbound" the arts and sciences become emblems of a temporarily redeemed civilization. In Aeschylus, Prometheus gives man not only fire, but makes possible man's development of many arts and crafts (vv. 445–71, 476–505), some of which do not involve fire (vv. 457 ff., 462 ff., 467 ff., 485 ff.). However, one may doubt whether, in Aeschylus, these crafts are emblems of civilization. Plato made the civil government, which Aeschylus's Prometheus failed to provide, the later gift of Zeus himself, perhaps reflecting developments in the latter parts of Aeschylus's trilogy. See *Protagoras*, 332e ff.; also Friedrich Solmsen, *Hesiod and Aeschylus* (Ithaca: Cornell University Press, 1949), pp. 138–46.

CHAPTER FIVE

1. The "Philosophical View of Reform" (1820), however, prescribes long-term remedies for social ills and does so with an air of confidence that contrasts sharply with the cyclic historical vision of "Hellas," dating from the next year. My concern, though, is with what I consider to be Shelley's most significant poetic productions, and there is no mistaking the decline of hope for sustained reform which these manifest after "The Revolt of Islam."

2. The use of pastoral elegy conventions is obvious, but Shelley's desertion of life's "trembling throng" in the last stanza is part of a general repudiation of conscious artistry and ultimately of art itself which can be traced through the latter stages of his career. The basis for this repudiation ("Flowers, ruins, statues, music, words are weak / The glory they transfuse with fitting truth to speak" [ll. 467–68]) is the conviction that life's dome of many-colored glass distorts transcendent reality into phenomenal illusion. See my article, "Shelley's Repudiation of Conscious Artistry," *English Studies in Canada* 1 (Spring 1975): 62–73.

3. Earl R. Wasserman, *Shelley: A Critical Reading* (Baltimore: Johns Hopkins University Press, 1971), pp. 484–85; Ross Woodman, *The Apocalyptic Vision in the Poetry of Shelley* (Toronto: University of Toronto Press, 1964), pp. xiii, 172. My discussion of Urania also reflects Woodman's argument.

4. Wasserman *(Shelley*, pp. 484–502) attempts to qualify it, but the violence of Shelley's tone ("eclipsing Curse of Birth," "repels to make thee wither") cannot be accommodated to his ingenious critical qualification. Nor can the denotative meaning of Shelley's statements in the concluding stanzas.

5. There is, as Woodman acknowledges (*The Apocalyptic Vision*, pp.

177–79), a suggestion of the demonic in the "dark" and "fearful" voyaging with which "Adonais" concludes.

6. "Defence of Poetry" in D. L. Clark, ed., in *Shelley's Prose or The Trumpet of a Prophecy* (Albuquerque: University of New Mexico Press, 1954), p. 294.

7. Ibid.

8. Ibid.

9. Ibid., pp. 294–95.

10. Ibid., p. 290.

11. Ibid., p. 282.

12. "Essay on Christianity," in ibid., p. 199 ff.; "Defence of Poetry," in ibid., p. 287 ff.

13. "Defence of Poetry," in ibid., p. 290.

14. Ibid., p. 297.

15. Ibid., p. 287.

16. W. H. Auden, "In Memory of W. B. Yeats," 2:36.

17. *Shelley: Poetical Works*, ed. Thomas Hutchinson, rev. G. M. Matthews, 2d ed. (London: Oxford University Press, 1970), p. 444.

18. White's account of the matter supports my own comments on the poem's biographical significance. Shelley was repeatedly attacked by the reviewers and, in White's opinion, saw himself as "completely ruined" by them. Besides this, however, his difficulties with the Lord Chancellor would alone be sufficient to motivate, and perhaps justify, his bitter and vindictive tone. See Newman Ivey White, *Shelley*, 2 vols. (New York: Knopf, 1940), 1:493–97, 2:296–97.

19. In a letter of 1821 to an unidentified lady Shelley says: "The French language you . . . already know; and if the great name of Rousseau did not redeem it, it would have been perhaps as well that you had remained entirely ignorant of it" (*Letters of Percy Bysshe Shelley*, ed. F. L. Jones, 2 vols. [Oxford: Clarendon Press, 1964], 2:278). Shelley also commends Rousseau in the "Defence": "He was essentially a poet. The others [Locke, Hume, Gibbon, Voltaire] were mere reasoners" (Clark, ed., *Shelley's Prose*, p. 292). Here Rousseau is definitely being considered as an "engaged" and inspired author.

20. I doubt if anyone would take issue with the following assertions: (1) that Rousseau was in no way influenced by the Orphic tradition which molded Shelley's transcendental aspiration; (2) that Rousseau saw Nature as God's handiwork, and an intense emotional response to natural impressions as a gateway to faith in God (*OEuvres*, 1:236, 388, 641–42, 1014); (3) that Rousseau emphasized the necessity for personal religious experience, through response to Nature, to other individuals, and, most importantly, to introspection, as essential to true faith (e.g., *Correspondance Complète*, 4:81, and especially *La Profession de Foi du Vicaire*

savoyard in *Émile*, book 4); (4) that Rousseau did not regard matter as a "stain" blotting out man's spiritual essence, nor love of the natural world as a bar to salvation. See Rousseau, *OEuvres Complètes*, ed. Bernard Gagnebin and Marcel Raymond, Pleiad Library, 4 vols. to date (Dijon: Gallimard, 1959–); Rousseau, *Correspondance Complète*, ed. R. A. Leigh, 33 vols.; vol. 4 (Geneva: Voltaire Foundation, 1967); Ronald Grimsley, *Rousseau and the Religious Quest* (London: Oxford University Press, 1968).

21. *Complete Works of Percy Bysshe Shelley*, ed. Roger Ingpen and Walter E. Peck, 10 vols. (New York: Gordian Press, 1965), 6:124, 130.

22. Rousseau, *OEuvres*, 2:471–87. In *La Nouvelle Heloise* Julie's garden at Clarens ("Elysium") is repeatedly described as an Eden and "if the physical nature of the Elysium is ultimately God's handiwork, it is Julie who animates . . . it . . . St. Preux cannot separate the physical elements of the Elysium from the presence of Julie's own being" (Grimsley, *Rousseau and the Religious Quest*, pp. 7, 105, 111).

23. Rousseau, *OEuvres*, 2:555 ff.

24. Grimsley, *Rousseau*, p. 21.

25. "The Triumph of Life," ll. 248–51 from Donald H. Reiman's text in his *Shelley's "The Triumph of Life": A Critical Study* (Urbana: University of Illinois Press, 1965).

26. See Charles E. Robinson, "The Shelley Circle and Coleridge's 'The Friend,'" *English Language Notes* 8 (June 1971): 269–74. Robinson advances several convincing arguments for Shelley's having read *The Friend* by 1816. One of these is the probable derivation of the Wordsworthian epigraph to "Alastor" from *The Friend* rather than directly from the 1814 *Excursion*. Robinson's excellent research lends strong support to Bloom, Tetreault, and other critics who, in one way or another, read Shelley's "Mont Blanc" in the light of Coleridge's "Hymn Before Sunrise" (published in *The Friend*). See Parks C. Hunter, Jr., "Coleridge's 'The Friend' as the Probable Source of the Wordsworth Quotation in the Preface to Shelley's 'Alastor,'" *Notes and Queries* 203 (1958): 474; Joseph Raben, "Coleridge as the Prototype of the Poet in Shelley's 'Alastor,'" *Review of English Studies* 17 (1966): 286–87; Harold Bloom, *Shelley's Mythmaking* (Ithaca: Cornell University Press, 1969), pp. 11–35; Ronald Tetreault, "Shelley and Byron Encounter the Sublime: Switzerland, 1816," *Revue Des Langues Vivantes* 41 (1975): 145–55.

27. Samuel Taylor Coleridge, *The Friend*, ed. Henry Nelson Coleridge, 3 vols. (London, 1844), First Landing Place, Essay one, 1:171–77, and especially Essay two, 1:189–91.

28. The definitions of *temper* which I supply here are strongly supported by the similar use of the term throughout Shelley's poetry. See F. S. Ellis, *A Lexical Concordance to the Poetical Works of Shelley* (London: Quaritch, 1892), p. 699.

29. *Letters*, ed., Jones, 1:84.

30. This is Coleridge's simplistic rendering of Rousseau's principle. *The Friend*, Section the First, Essay Four, 1:262–63.

31. Ibid., pp. 265, 270–71.

32. Ibid., p. 265.

33. Whether or not this is actually true in the final historical analysis has been the subject of much debate. But, even in his own lifetime, Rousseau felt his works were misunderstood and distorted out of all proportion by the French. His relation to Marx, to totalitarianism, and other aspects of his extensive influence are not as immediately relevant to my argument as his own attitude to the French public. See *Rousseau Juge de Jean Jacques*, in *OEuvres*, 1:932.

34. See White, *Shelley*, 1:203–42, 491–97. From the difficulties and failures attendant upon his humanitarian efforts in Ireland and Wales to the use of "Queen Mab" as legal evidence of his immorality, Shelley's life seemed, to him at least, a constant struggle against public apathy and blindly dogmatic authority.

35. *Letters*, ed., Jones, 1:433.

36. *Mary Shelley's Journal*, ed. F. L. Jones (Norman: University of Oklahoma Press, 1947), p. 72.

37. Rousseau, of course, regarded a solitary natural setting as the most fitting for spiritual and intellectual growth. This sentiment is reflected, not only in *Émile*, but throughout this work, and individual citation would be supererogatory.

CHAPTER SIX

1. See Earl R. Wasserman's study of "Adonais" in *Shelley: A Critical Reading* (Baltimore: Johns Hopkins University Press, 1971), pp. 462–502.

2. Shelley's quest for eternity is not necessarily a search for escape through transcendence or death, as some scholars (e.g., Woodman) have implied, but rather a quest for certain knowledge. Doubtless, as "Adonais" shows, Shelley considered the possibility that death might be the gateway to enlightenment. However, "The Triumph of Life," like the sonnet "Lift Not the Painted Veil," suggests that Shelley's final attitude to this possibility was one of extreme skepticism. See Ross Woodman, "The Triumph of Life" in *The Apocalyptic Vision in the Poetry of Shelley* (Toronto: University of Toronto Press, 1964), pp. 194, 196–97.

3. Harold Bloom, *Shelley's Mythmaking* (Ithaca: Cornell University Press, 1969), p. 220. While insisting that the poem does not repudiate the validity of Shelley's earlier visions, Bloom nevertheless sees in "The Triumph of Life" the defeat of Shelley's attempt to humanize the universe through the creation of a unique and individual myth. My own

position is that "The Triumph of Life" is the poetic portrayal of a skeptic's failed quest for ultimate certainty.

4. Ibid., pp. 220–75; P. H. Butter, "Sun and Shape in Shelley's 'The Triumph of Life,'" *Review of English Studies*, 13 (1962): 40–51; W. Cherubini, "Shelley's Own Symposium: 'The Triumph of Life,'" *Studies in Philology* 39 (1942): 559–70; G. M. Matthews, "On Shelley's 'The Triumph of Life,'" *Studia Neophilologica* 34 (1962): 105–34; Adel Salama, *Shelley's Major Poems: A Reinterpretation* (Salzburg: Institute of English Studies, University of Salzburg, 1973), pp. 273–94; F. Melian Stawell, "Shelley's 'The Triumph of Life,'" *Essays and Studies by Members of the English Association, Oxford* 5 (1914): 304–30; Donald H. Reiman, *Shelley's "The Triumph of Life": A Critical Study* (Urbana: University of Illinois Press, 1965), pp. 19–116.

5. Glenn O'Malley provides a perceptive, if limited, examination of the imagery in the last chapter of his *Shelley and Synesthesia* (Evanston: Northwestern University Press, 1964).

6. Donald Reiman *(Shelley's "The Triumph of Life,"* p. 34) takes issue with critics who severely limit the number who escape life's dominion, but it makes no difference to my reading how large or small the number may be.

7. Woodman, in the last chapter of his book, defines it in the terms of Orphic Platonism. Bloom attacks this approach, although Woodman's argument is, in this instance anyway, convincing.

8. All quotations from "The Triumph of Life" in this chapter are from Reiman's text (see n. 4), the most thoroughly researched text available. Quotations in this chapter from other Shelley poems are from *Shelley: Poetical Works*, ed. Thomas Hutchinson, rev. G. M. Matthews, 2d ed. (London: Oxford University Press, 1970). A point-by-point comparison of the Matthews, Reiman, and Hutchinson texts has raised no crucial problems for me, since I am concerned here with the total pattern of the imagery, not with the biographical implications of particular word-choices (as Matthews sometimes is). Nor does my argument hinge on the precise definition of any one episode's thematic significance, but rather on the poetic development and transformation of images which all three editors include in their texts. See G. M. Matthews, "'The Triumph of Life': A New Text," *Studia Neophilologica* 32 (1960): 271–309.

9. Notably by A. C. Bradley, in "Notes on Shelley's 'The Triumph of Life,'" *Modern Language Review* 9 (1914): 441–56.

10. See Bloom's comments on Bradley's article. Bloom, *Shelley's Mythmaking*, p. 225.

11. See ibid., p. 224, and Bradley, "Notes on 'Triumph of Life,'" p. 444. Bloom emphasizes the need to explore the sun's function in the poem, rather than allegorize it by reference to other works. I am trying to

explore its significance both in the poem and in the context of earlier work which Shelley deliberately echoes.

12. Wasserman (*Shelley*, pp. 462–502) conclusively demonstrates this transformation in "Adonais."

13. The influence of Petrarch's *Trionfi* has also been frequently noted. See Milton Wilson, *Shelley's Later Poetry* (New York: Columbia University Press, 1959), pp. 283–91.

14. Both the sunrise of lines 1 to 20 and the Wordsworthian echoes in Rousseau's narrative parody the idea of time as a purgatorial agent.

15. Perhaps also the third canto of "Don Juan" (3.104.6–8): "My altars are the mountains and the Ocean, / Earth—air—stars,—all that springs from the great Whole, / Who hath produced, and will receive the Soul." Re Coleridge see Bloom, *Shelley's Mythmaking*, pp. 11–19.

16. This is, of course, not an original observation. See Matthews, "On Shelley's 'The Triumph of Life,'" p. 106.

17. Cf. "the car's creative ray" (l. 533) and the similarly "all-miscreative brain of Jove" ("Prometheus Unbound," 1:448).

18. The shape has caused considerable contention. She is obviously beautiful and obviously recalls the benevolent female deities of Shelley's earlier poems. Yet her gift of nepenthe seems destructive in its effect upon Rousseau. What is to be done with this? Baker and Matthews, among others, suggest that Rousseau brings his destruction upon himself, either by not drinking the nepenthe at all or by not drinking it to the dregs. Bloom and Butter find this ridiculous. See Carlos Baker, *Shelley's Major Poetry: The Fabric of a Vision* (Princeton: Princeton University Press, 1948), pp. 264–67; G. M. Matthews, "On Shelley's 'The Triumph of Life,'" pp. 113, 116–17; Bloom, *Shelley's Mythmaking*, p. 269; Butter, "Sun and Shape," p. 46. It is clear, however, that Rousseau did at least touch the cup with his lips (l. 104) and that this act precipitated the subsequent erasure of his thought. But the essential point of contention is this: is the shape good or bad? The position of this essay is that she is neither; that her true significance cannot be defined. The point of the poem is this very uncertainty: like the other seeming realities in Rousseau's world, the shape cannot be truly known and identified. Reiman sees the shape as a second "Alastor" dream-maiden and, to the extent that her true nature is unknowable, this is an astute observation. But Reiman is less convincing on the shape's actual value and significance because of his tendentious attempt to see *all* Shelley's work as hopeful (pp. 69–72). For the westward movement of the shape see Stawell, "Shelley's 'The Triumph of Life,'" p. 112 and n. 1.

19. See O'Malley, *Shelley and Synesthesia*, pp. 75–88 and his chapter "Melody of Light" generally.

20. See also Bloom's comments on the ironic parallel between the

shape and Dante's Matilda. Bloom, *Shelley's Mythmaking*, pp. 242, 271.

21. The "public way" resembles the "broad highway of the world" in "Epipsychidion" and parodies the "true way" of the New Testament or the *Pilgrim's Progress*. The various fates of the people on the public way, especially with Rousseau's falling "by the wayside" (l. 541), surely recall the parable of the sower. See Bloom, ibid., p. 227.

22. See "Defence of Poetry" in D. L. Clark, ed., *Shelley's Prose or The Trumpet of a Prophecy* (Albuquerque: University of New Mexico Press, 1954), p. 295. My treatment of the chariot was prompted by Woodman's perceptive comments. See Woodman, *The Apocalyptic Vision*, pp. 185–86.

23. "Defence of Poetry," in Clark, ed., *Shelley's Prose*, p. 295.

24. Ibid., p. 172.

INDEX